CAT RAINCOCK

Born To Shine

The Modern Woman's
Guide to a Happier Life

hey,

Welcome to this wonderful book brought to you by
That Guy's House Publishing.

At That Guy's House we believe in real and raw wellness
books that inspire the reader from a place of authenticity
and honesty.

This book has been carefully crafted by both the author and
publisher with the intention that it will bring you a glimmer of
hope, a rush of inspiration and sensation of inner peace.

It is our hope that you thoroughly enjoy this book and pass it
onto friends who may also be in need of a glimpse into their
own magnificence.

Have a wonderful day.

Love,

Sean Patrick

That Guy.

☆

For Poppy,

The original crew member.

Always by my side with

unconditional love.

Together through it all.

Souls aligned.

Forever and always in my heart.

GRATITUDE LIST

Thank you to the following; you have all played a part in my journey and, as a result, this book. I'm so grateful for you. My heart is full, I am blessed.

☆ *To my inner child* – We did it! We faced our fears and took on the world.

☆ *To my self-esteem* – What a great team we make! Here is to more adventures.

☆ *Adam* – Boy, we have grown and so has my heart for you! I love you deeply.

☆ *Jake & Elodie* – For being my greatest teachers. I love you. Lalu Wadu.

☆ *Mum & Dad* – For my journey and creating me! I love you both.

☆ *Nick & Chris* - For being my dear brothers.

☆ *Michelle Zelli* – Thank you for cracking me open and showing me the way.

☆ *Marisa Peer* – Thank you for sharing your tools.

☆ *For all my friends, old and new, family near and far* – You have all contributed in some way to this book and my life journey.

☆ *To You, the Readers* – For allowing me to share my tools with you and gifting me the opportunity to change your life. Every story I hear from you reminds me why I share my story with other women, so that you can live your greatest, happiest and most fulfilled life.

CONTENTS

☆

'This book will *change* your life,
when you make the *commitment*
to yourself to heal and welcome
transformation.'

THIS IS MY CALL TO YOU

There has never been a better time
to stand up and be counted.
Women are rising and so must you.
Show the world your gifts because the world is waiting.
You were born with a message, a talent, a job to do.
Don't let time pass you by without sharing it.

You have played small for far too long,
hidden your true self.
Your confidence has been quashed.
But as of today, that changes.
We are igniting your confidence.
Giving you back the belief in yourself
So that you can shine your light and make a difference.

Do this for you, your sisters, mother, daughters
and for every young girl out there.
As you empower yourself, you empower others.
Lead by example, have courage, be brave.

Rise up, sweet one. You are magic.
Shine your light. The planet needs you.

You were born to shine.

Shine on, Sister.

MAKING THIS BOOK
WORK FOR YOU

HEY SISTER! YEAH YOU!

Low self-esteem is endemic in modern society. Did you know that 60 to 80% of women in the UK and US suffer from low self-esteem? That's up to four out of five of your friends who feel inadequate. What the bleep! It is a shocking statistic. I'm sure that even if you are struggling with low self-esteem, that will surprise you too, but equally it's good to know you're not alone. I was one of those women and it's my duty to you and all our sisters out there to change this. There is no manual for life, no guide to achieving that unconditional blissful life, but there is this book. You have picked this up because part of you (your soul) knows deep down that you need to heal and repair those disconnected parts of you so that you can live a whole-hearted life and return to viewing yourself with high self-esteem. Enough of this 'not enoughness', enough of this feeling of not mattering and feeling unimportant. You deserve so much more, and in this book I show you why you deserve more and how you can create a life you love. Yes, you! You create the life. Just like when you walk around the supermarket choosing what you make for dinner, you can choose how the rest of your life looks and feels.

Whether you are a new mum feeling overwhelmed, a woman embarking on her career and feeling not enough, an experienced mother who has lost herself, a business woman stressed with life's challenges, a woman who has chosen to be child free or has a childless existence and is feeling frustrated with life, a sister, a friend, an aunt, a daughter – these words are for you. Yummy mummy, lifestyle junky or entrepreneur, I know you are ready to dip your toe into the spiritual pond. This book is dedicated to the women who are looking for transformation and are ready to do the work on themselves. I am merely the facilitator, the light that shines the way, the mentor – it's your strength, focus and tenacity that will bring you the worthwhile results.

Do you wake up in the morning with a niggling feeling in your stomach, with a sense there must be more to life than what you have? Do you feel like whatever you achieve isn't enough? Do you feel overwhelmed with life? Are your emotions taking over and stopping you from fulfilling your dreams and goals? If you have answered yes to any of these, this book is for you. In three simple steps, this book will help you understand why you feel like you do, help you to face your fears and give you the tools to rebuild your self-esteem and consequently your life. After you have read this book you will feel more confident, lighter, brighter and, overall, ready to shine your light and show the world your true gifts. It's time to take you on a journey of discovery and transformation. Why? Because you deserve a full and happy life. Happiness may have been pedestalled and feel like an unachievable goal and something that everyone else has. But you can have it too if you take my three steps. The first step is to discover, or should I say rediscover, your magnificence. The second step is to change your outlook and the way you see life. And finally, once you have taken those first two steps you can take the third, which is to create a life you love.

This book is based on my three-step journey and the process I went through. I took these very steps and here I am now writing a book, travelling the world, spreading my message far and wide and supporting women to stand up and step into their greatness. I never thought I would do or have anything of these things I have now; and I don't mean financial things – I mean the free things like joy, love, happiness and, at times, bliss. If I can do it, so can you.

If you're just like me, then you're at a point in your life where you have made the big career move, got the job, got the house, got married or found your life partner, had babies, or chosen not to, and you are searching for the next move, your next step, because what you have isn't enough. You have an empty feeling, but, in daring to feel there should be more, you feel conflicted because what you have should be enough. Society and the mass media have led you to believe that if you tick the correct boxes, you will be happy. You are asking yourself, 'What now?' You feel lost, unfulfilled, frustrated, and this niggle isn't going away.

You're looking for change, I can feel it in my bones, so that you can achieve your dreams and share the gifts that you were put on this planet to do. You have got to that point in your life where what you have just isn't enough and you want to try something new because the old isn't working anymore. I hear you. Now, this might seem like a far-fetched idea at this moment in time – I thought the same. I didn't believe I could change my life. I didn't know I could transform the way I thought. I certainly didn't subscribe to the idea that I could create a life that I not only chose but loved. And yet, it's true. I did exactly that and so can you.

<u>MY MISSION</u>

My mission is to empower women and I'm starting with you. I want to show you there is another way, that you don't have to be 'damaged' to seek therapy or healing. Everyone is entitled to a big life upgrade. My story is here to show women that there is hope, you do matter and there is more to life than what you are experiencing. I'm going to give you tools to change your life for the better. You deserve to have the life you dreamt of as a child and to fulfil your potential, to rid yourself of self-limiting beliefs, to be happy, free, living with passion and purpose. It's time to align your life so that you can become the woman you were meant to be before the world told you who you should be. I was an ordinary girl

who learnt some key things and now live an extraordinary life. I have manifested my dream life and have achieved, and continue to achieve, more than I could have wished for. My self-limiting beliefs were stifling me. I was running the same thought patterns and behaviours over and over. I was stuck, trapped and suffocated under the blanket of life.

Time to take your ordinary existence and make it extraordinary. Yay baby, I have goose bumps just thinking about it.

☆ SHOPPING ALERT! ☆

Pop down to your local stationers and buy yourself a journal to note down your journey. This will help you to document how far you have come and to look back at how you navigated and coped through a trigger or two. It is a reminder of what helped and healed you. We are so conditioned to avoid praising ourselves so this gives you an opportunity to look over your initial discoveries and self-limiting beliefs and see how they have changed. And of course, this is where you set your intention and focus on the life you want to create.

Throughout this book, I urge you to ask yourself the following:

☆ What have I discovered?

☆ What do I want to change?

☆ What do I want to create?

LOOK INTO MY EYES

As well as a heap load of information, tips, tools, love and light, there are some free guided meditations for you as you work through this book. You can find them at the back of this book in the book resources section. They are there for you to use to embed change and encourage creation. I talk more about the power of hypnosis later in the book but as a trained clinical hypnotherapist, I guarantee you these guided meditations are a mini super tool and the easiest homework you can have.

Sit back. listen and change.

THE THREE STEPS

In this book, I guide you through three simple steps to making you matter. In the first step, we explore the self-limiting beliefs you have that are affecting your self-esteem, self-worth and ultimately your self-confidence. I will give you exercises and tools to let them go.

Then we move on to understanding your mind and how you can rewire it to be the version of yourself you want to be. Hypnosis and guided meditations were a key part of my healing and I continue to use them in my life to ensure my mind doesn't play any naughty tricks. I show you why and how it works.

And finally, Step 3 is all about the magic. By this stage in the book, you will have a good idea of what you have been feeling and thinking and you'll have reprogrammed your mind; this is where the real fun happens when you can truly create some serious transformation.

step one – discover

Most of your adult feelings and behaviours are dictated by events in your childhood – these can be small and seem insignificant but they can have a big impact. This step is dedicated to returning to the root of your low self-esteem. This step uncovers the painful events and experiences you had as a child and links them to the self-limiting beliefs by integrating and dealing with them in a purposeful way, turning them into sources of power and knowledge for growth. When you understand the emotions and negative responses you have developed to specific situations and memories, you can change them. When you feel it, you can heal it.

step two - change

This step is all about change, and with your new-found knowledge about your past and how it has shaped your present, this step will help you understand your mind and get acquainted with your own computer software (subconscious mind) so that you can re-programme it to hold positive thoughts, new beliefs and ultimately change the way you think, feel and act so that you can achieve your goals and aspirations.

step three - create

This step is all about creating. Following the rewiring of your mind and clearing out of old emotions and beliefs, you have made space for new, high vibration emotions such as joy and love. When you vibrate at a higher rate, you can begin to create the life you want. In this step, you will learn the science behind the Law of Attraction and learn simple tools to creating the life you want based on your new ways of thinking and feeling.

MAGIC AWAITS

This book will change your life when you make that commitment to yourself to heal and welcome transformation. You've heard the saying before, 'no pain, no gain' – and that's it. You have to feel to heal and sometimes that will feel uncomfortable and at times dreadfully messy. Let me tell you this, it's meant to. There will be moments in this book when old memories and feelings may be triggered; trust this is just the way it is meant to be. Ensure you have a good support system around you to share what's come up and if you need to, seek the advice of a professional. Remember, we aren't used to feeling, only numbing feelings out with a glass or three of wine, social media or television to name just a few. The idea of this book is to uncover the past and that can bring painful memories to the surface. But when you set your intention to heal and move forward in life, this pain is temporary and there is always huge growth when we sit in the pain, breathe through it and honour the feelings coming up. For everyone who purchases this book, you become part of an exclusive Facebook group where I support your growth and am here to help you navigate through. You can also follow me on Instagram where I love hearing from you and giving you daily encouragement and support from the sidelines. Either way, you will have a community of like-minded women who hold space for you and support your growth too. Those feelings have been suppressed for far too long, darling.

So however we may meet, this is the starting point of a beautiful and alchemy-filled journey together and I can't wait to begin.

**Remember this mantra: I am strong,
I can do this, I am ready to feel so I can heal.**

ONE LAST THING

Before you go any further, I urge you to set an intention. Something, someone, somewhere, somehow, this book has arrived in your hands. It was meant to be – me and you – how beautiful! And deep inside you there is a reason why this magnificent coincidence and crossing of paths has arisen. There is something you want to change, even if you don't know it just yet. You're being called to let go of something (or some things – let's not put limits on it) no longer serving you. What is that thing? What comes to mind first? What do you want to change in your life but don't have the confidence (just yet) to do it? Well, make that your clear intention right here, right now.

☆ *I am ready to discover* ....

☆ *I am ready to change* ....

☆ *I am ready to create* ....

And you're off!! Intention set. Seatbelts on. Sparkles on their way!

Ready?

Let's do this, Sister!

Hashtag at the ready – **#borntoshinebook**

☆

'Without the trials
and tribulations,
I wouldn't be here now.
My story has made me.'

I am...

I am not an actress, a junkie, a girl
with a big traumatic tale to tell.
I'm not from an aristocratic background
or born in to a spiritual family.
I am me and that's my story.

I am an ordinary girl.
No frills, no leg up, no past.
I am real. I am authentic.
Telling a tangible and honest story.
My story is here to help you.

I have taken my ordinary life &
made it extraordinary.
I'm a down to earth girl
Now living an out of this world existence.

I am me and that's enough.
I am me and that's my greatest strength.

Who are you?

ME AND MY STORY

ME – THE FUNDAMENTALS

Before we go any further, let me introduce myself and tell you a bit about me. After all, we're about to spend over 200 pages together, side by side, so it seems only right I share my story first. Here goes. I am 40 years young (at the time of writing this book). I am a wife, and a mother of two children. I'm a London girl, born and bred, but have a very special place in my heart for my spiritual home, Glastonbury, where I went to school from 9 until the ripe old age of 18. I have two older brothers, and my parents are still married after more than 50 years together and live less than a mile down the road from me in London.

I am a fully qualified clinical hypnotherapist and was trained by Marisa Peer, one of the world's leading hypnotherapists. I practise her method, RTT (Rapid Transformational Therapy). I embarked on my personal transformation with Michelle Zelli, leading psycho-spiritual coach, and am a devout follower of her work after my transformation under her watch. I am still mentored and coached by Michelle.

Prior to my career change at 35 years old, I was a television presenter. I formerly worked in sport television for seven years at Sky Sports and Chelsea TV as a presenter and reporter. I moved on to working in an entirely different vocation, and trained as an interior designer and worked on various projects until I called it a day and became a mum.

I have a creative and artistic eye, I am a flexitarian – I mostly eat plant food and always organic. I'm a clean living kind of chick, and I like to think of myself as consciously aware, passionate about the planet and, most importantly, I love dogs and am mum to one 15-year-old miniature schnauzer called Poppy.

BEHIND THE SCENES

Now let's get to the nitty gritty. At 35, life looked good from the outside. I had a beautiful husband and two wonderful children and a lovely home in central London. I had ticked all the boxes. But that was a far cry from how I felt inside and the heart-shaped box that resided in my chest wasn't ticked or filled up.

I had dreamt of being married and having kids all of my life but when it came to the crunch, I was desperately unfulfilled. I was an angry mother, a resentful wife, an overly sensitive friend, a dependent daughter and a needy sister. I thought this was how life was meant to be and didn't know any other way. *Life's hard, suck it up, what have you got to be upset about* was the narrative. What was wrong with me? Why did I feel like this when I had everything I dreamt of? That was the moment I turned my ordinary life into an extraordinary one.

I was, and still am in many ways, an ordinary girl, who up until 35 was living a very ordinary life. Little did I realise that my relatively uneventful childhood (or so it seemed) had taken a massive toll on my self-esteem and self-worth. This is how my childhood looked: a house in central London, a 2-point 4 family unit, two older brothers, parents still together, a father in the film industry and an actress for a mother (sounds way more glamorous or extraordinary than it was). What more could you ask for? Although having my children was the trigger that sent me over the edge, it had been a slow downward spiral before their arrival. My children just sparked the impending breakdown a little early; it was the bun in the pressure cooker that eventually led to my breakthrough following my breakdown. Looking back on life before kids, I was functioning in survival mode and only coping by accepting a damaged version of myself and my life.

The reality was, I felt abandoned, not lovable, inadequate: I felt I didn't matter. My parents' busy careers left little time for me: I was largely looked after by nannies and au pairs and when I was with my parents, they weren't entirely present. Mum, in addition to her acting career, had a house to run (no online supermarket back then), three kids to manage and not forgetting the two dogs. My Dad, who had lost his parents at an early age, had learnt to survive on his own and lived a very independent life and that was still the case despite having three children.

Some may judge my life and say that because I seemingly had so much — a financially stable upbringing, a home, married parents and attended a great school — my life and I were anything but ordinary. And the truth is, yes, my life looked great on paper but it didn't give me what I needed and despite all of those things I still struggled with low self-esteem. This is about having trauma as an adult despite having no big trauma as a child. This is about achieving what society and the media say we 'should' have and it not being enough. This is about the shame I carried for having a privileged childhood, yet still feeling empty. The fact is, I have suffered trauma and self-esteem failure despite the type of childhood I had and I discovered tools that transcended my ordinary existence. You see, low self-esteem doesn't discriminate. It doesn't matter what you have, who you are, where you are from, what clothes you wear, whether you are rich or poor, or whether or not your parents did a good or a bad job at bringing you up. You can have all of those things or none of them and still feel the same pain and emptiness deep down inside. Why? Because somewhere along the line, your needs weren't met and you formed a belief that you didn't matter and that you weren't enough and that belief is still with you today.

At 31, after years of kissing frogs and desperately trying to keep up with society's model of happiness – HAPPINESS = HOUSE, HUSBAND, KIDS (a model that's incorrect, by the way) – I found my man, my prince, my hero and had two children. I had my son at 35 and my daughter two years later. It was then my world started to fall apart despite this being the best part of my life so far. Where was the fairy tale of motherhood? All I felt was overwhelmed and broken. I was overflowing with anger and resentment, and I couldn't let go of control. I was a perfectionist in everything I did (making kids' birthday cakes, hosting parties at our house and insisting on doing the catering, cooking and cleaning when I had a three-month-old baby and still breastfeeding). I wrote list after list of what I needed to achieve each day in order to feel 'enough' but I never accomplished my endless lists and therefore never felt enough, only frustrated and always at myself. I had a compulsion to do and to be everything that came my way. I never said no, only yes. I had to be everything to everyone, the perfect mum, perfect wife, doting daughter, strong and supportive friend. I stretched myself so far, across so many things, between too many people, that eventually I snapped.

My husband turned to me one day and asked me, 'Are you happy?' My reply was 'Yes, of course, I'm just stressed, I have two kids and I'm trying to do everything.' The truth was, I wasn't happy; deep down, I was very sad and very lost. This was the start of my journey back to me. For me, the trigger was my children but whether I had kids or not, I was ready to pop. They were simply the catalyst that prompted the meltdown. They were in fact my greatest gift: my son had brought up all my issues to heal, and my daughter's arrival confirmed the work I needed to do on myself.

It was time for a massive self-esteem revamp.

I went on a mission to transform myself, my life, my world, and these are the tools I give you in this book. My journey wasn't a bed of roses and certainly it wasn't easy; it took great courage and perseverance but I knew life couldn't continue as it was. I was ready to make the change. Are you? I wanted a different future than the one I was carving out. Do you?

MY OLD PROGRAMMING

My career-driven parents worked in creative industries so Dad was often on film locations, while Mum could be found headlining on stage in the West End. Much of my time was either spent alone, which naturally lent itself to mountains of time creating my own stories, fantasies and fairy tales, or I was with nannies. I was a naturally creative child, as we all are until it gets withered down. I told myself story after story about why Mum and Dad were or weren't there by my side which led to me forming simple but destructive beliefs such as *I don't matter, if I did Mum and Dad would be here. I'm not lovable, if I was Mum and Dad would be here.* These stories were the subtext but eventually they became the subtext to an over-riding headline: *I am not enough because if I was, Mum and Dad would be here.*

THE CAVEAT

This was never about whether Mum or Dad did a good or a bad job, whether they were right or whether they were wrong. It simply was how it was. Yes, my needs weren't met but we all come into this life with wounds passed down through lifetimes, lineages, soul contracts that need healing, we all pick up self-limiting beliefs from someone, somewhere, even if our parents were wonderful. There is no 'perfect childhood' but there is a perfectly imperfect way as an adult to remedy and change what went before. With this in mind, whatever you discover in this book about what beliefs you have created and where they came from, this isn't a witch hunt for your parents. It is simply an understanding of what went before and what needs to be changed in order to create the life you want now.

Choose now as the time to do it. Say yes to the upgrade. The repercussions are huge, not just for you but for the people in your life. Did you know that our wounds carry down five generations until they are healed? You are making the first step today while reading this book to let go of your limiting beliefs so that your daughters, daughters' daughters, god-daughter, nieces and friends can see the change in you. We must set an example to the children of this world, our sisters, our friends, colleagues and acquaintances and be the beacon of light that this planet needs. Lead by example; *as you rise, we all rise*, as Rebecca Campbell so beautifully shares.

PLAYING SMALL

I learnt from an early age to play small. What do I mean by this? Well, in simple terms, to hide myself and to play down my magnificence. I believed it wasn't safe to show my true self. I was the youngest sibling, one of three, the only girl. For some, that meant that I was favoured for my uniqueness; I mean this in the loosest sense, unique as in the only girl. Sometimes I was, sometimes it played in my favour as I often needed rescuing from a situation – you know like when you need bailing out financially, or arms to fall into when you have broken up with a boyfriend and can't hero yourself. And then, of course, there were the jobs that I couldn't stand doing and I would run to my parents to give me the sign off to quit. You see, by inheriting the label of youngest I played the role very well as the youngest, smallest and most vulnerable. Not because I was, just because I had assumed my role, and I continued to need rescuing way into adulthood. I had learnt early to play the damsel in distress. It got me connection but it sure didn't help me – not that I knew it at the time.

With two older brothers, one eight years older than me and the other three years older, it was enough of a gap for us to have few bonds between us as there was little time all together to form deep bonds. They were busy playing sport or playing up and there was no time for their little sister. Cue feelings of loneliness, disconnection, being not lovable and generally being the annoying little sister. Why didn't they love me for me? I can't help it, I'm young, a girl and I am the way I am. Stay small, stay away, stay safe. The narrative continued. Truth is, this was never about me, but I had made it all about me. This later manifested in feelings of being 'annoying' and 'uninteresting' with other men. It formed part of the mis-belief that I had created around men. I was always in long-term relationships. I picked up boyfriends who weren't terribly interested in me or faithful for that matter, which of course fed in to my 'not enoughness' and lack of true connection with boys (Dad and brothers).

My school days were mildly eventful, I went to boarding school in Glastonbury (my spiritual home) at nine years old. It was a place I loved dearly and have fond memories of despite being terribly homesick for the first couple of years. I loved it because I had connection, care and my needs were met, so at times it felt better than being unseen and unheard at home. That said, I missed my Mum a lot and longed for her time and attention. Abandonment was another story I had told myself, even though Mum had always said I could come home if I hated it. I never did; sisterhood and comradery outweighed home in London. Thankfully here, I excelled at sport and gained confidence in the classroom and made some wonderful friends who are still in my life today.

WHERE'S MY STAGE?

Actresses long to be seen, loved and appreciated. I longed
for this and therefore longed to be an actress too. To see my
Mum on TV, in films and on stage was inspiring. I remember
watching her with pride gushing from my heart as she tapped
her way through *Stepping Out* in the West End. Trouble was,
with the stories and beliefs I had formed as a child, it meant
I had big shoes to fill and little 'enoughness' to fill them. I
remember my first time on stage: it was my first ballet show. I
was not yet four years old and my teacher couldn't even get me
to walk on stage, and when she finally did, I sat at the front
crying throughout. Then there was my first stint in the West
End as a six-year-old, when my Saturday acting school put on
Pinocchio; I cried the whole way through that too. How could
I be like Mum and fill her tap shoes? My early formulation of
beliefs was hindering me already and I was dulling my shine
because I felt like there was no room to shine.

I embarked on a career at Sky Sports as I wanted to be a sports
presenter, my modern version of an actress. I also knew that
by working in sport, I would get connection with my Dad:
he loved football and particularly Chelsea. I got my first
screen test but when it came to reading the autocue, I was
like a rabbit in headlights. No surprise, I didn't get the call
up. This dead end led me to pursue a life at Chelsea Football
Club (note the pursuit of sports-based jobs). I later learnt this
industry was giving me connection with my father rather than

a genuine love for it; although I did feel like I loved it at the time, it wasn't my soul's calling. It wasn't long before I quit that path and embarked on a career in interior design, another link to Dad, who when he wasn't busy in the film industry was renovating properties. I qualified, and I loved it and the creative process that came with it. Drawing was, and still is, a creative passion of mine. I thought I had found 'my thing' until I got on the building site (the stage) and found myself barking and directing orders at builders for not reading the drawings – feelings of 'not heard' were rife. Truth is, the builders were just representing the feelings I had at home as a kid – not heard, not seen – and they were coming up all over again. I didn't stay long in this career, my frustrations grew, and my feelings of insignificance continued to erode my confidence and belief in myself. There was definitely a pattern of giving up when the going got tough, which was all linked to not truly believing in my ability to stick it out through the rough times – cue the negative self-talk, which would inevitably help me make excuses and come up with lots of stories about why I should quit or, rather, give up.

HERE'S MY FAIRY TALE

So here I was. Careers that hadn't filled me up. Failed long-term relationships under my belt. What next? By 31, I met my husband to be, who was genuinely the knight in shining armour I had dreamt of. I had found the chosen one, I just needed the ring and the babies and all would be swell – as society told me. Or so I thought – I believed that if I found the one, got married and had children life would be tip top.

MOTHERHOOD

I loved being pregnant, I felt whole. The joy and bliss of my first few days as a mum were overwhelming in a good way, but also in a less good way. We were so happy to have a healthy baby boy. I remember the morning after the emergency caesarean birth, I woke up, so happy to have my baby in my arms but I felt like a little girl, overwhelmed and tearful about how on earth I would manage to take care of this amazing little being. Those feelings of being overwhelmed never really left me and I was, as many of us are, a fearful, neurotic and controlling mother who was fixated on routine, which I was led to believe a baby likes in order to feel safe, but I liked it too. It kept me safe. I knew what I had to do and when to do it. I had felt so out of control as a kid that I needed to control life around me to feel safe; and as an adult, I was doing this with my son. I had also been so overwhelmed with emotions as a child but had found ways to push the feelings down; but they surfaced when I gave birth and as an adult I was overwhelmed by everything – the daily routine, a crying baby, what to feed him, what not to feed him, what medicine to give him or not, and so on. I muddled through with unconditional love for my son, doing the best I could, running on my little-girl-lost programming.

What next? I still felt empty. Ahhh, we forgot to get married. Let's do that and then we'll have another baby. A fairy tale wedding followed by baby number two. A beautiful little girl. Now we had one of both. Tick, tick, fist pump! Now I really have ticked the boxes. Surely I must be happy now! A year went by, I continued to muddle through on my strict routine and rigid timetables. And then I went pop.

I could not keep it together anymore. They say meltdowns or midlife crises can be brought on by a death, a divorce or a house move. Well, mine was a birth, but retrospectively, it was my rebirth. My daughter triggered a tsunami of old memories that left me broken and lost and very empty. I was full up with what I had, but deeply empty inside. Fear and control reigned, while playing small kept me safe and away from harm, but it was only a matter of time before the activities I had used to numb out pain – career changes, drama-filled relationships, exercise, shopping, more drama and so on – would come crumbling to a halt. It was time to look at myself and rediscover me. And so I did, and I live to tell the tale.

There was no big trauma, just needs that were unintentionally not met and this was the story I had created and the beliefs that I had adopted. The journey of creation was quite plain to see.

So there I was with a list of self-limiting beliefs.

I felt...

Lonely

Abandoned

Neglected

Betrayed

Not heard

Not seen

Not enough

Not lovable

Like I don't matter.

Thankfully, I no longer hold these beliefs. I believe in me.
I am none of the above, I never was. I now know that I am
enough and as a result, life mirrors back my new beliefs.

LIFE NOW

As I sit here writing this chapter, I feel blessed for how my
story unfolded. Without the trials and tribulations, I wouldn't
be where I am now. My story has made me. It was all so
perfectly aligned and thought out. I'm a better coach because
I have been there and done it. I have a natural ability to speak
on stage following my time on TV. I have a natural confidence
and love of the spotlight because I have seen Mum do it so well.

Do I feel let down by my parents? No, they are a product of
their parents, they did their best. Do I feel betrayed by my
brothers for not loving me like I wished they had? No, they
had their own story and life to heal. I wouldn't change a single
thing about my past and am truly thankful I have had the

opportunity to heal and let go of so much this lifetime. Here's to enlightenment – I'm hoping it's coming in the next life!

Life isn't meant to be perfect and calm all the time and if this is what you are trying to achieve then you are barking up the wrong tree. This is about the start of giving back to yourself, meeting your needs and having the tools to live a happy life. There will be moments in life when you will get knocked down and winded, but as you continue through this book you will know how to cope with them and come out the other side unscathed.

This is how I live my life now: imagine life like an open expanse of water, some days it is calm, other days the waves are big, the water is choppy, and sometimes a huge storm has taken hold and you're struggling to keep your head above water, let alone your boat! I teach you how to navigate your boat to calmer waters. When you look back at where the self-limiting beliefs come from, you will gain a deep understanding of yourself and your past, and that allows you to move through life peacefully towards your future.

I'm on the other side now of the intense emotions, the suffocating negative self-talk and the endless list of failures. I made a commitment to myself to grow, to smash goals I never knew were possible. Every day, I'm learning something new and peeling away another layer of old programming. I now set myself bigger goals and continue to amaze myself at how free and liberated I feel now that I have let go of so many old fears, emotions and self-limiting beliefs. I am so grateful for the lessons and very proud that I am now functioning as my authentic self, living the life I dreamt of. I deserve it, I matter and so do you.

☆

'There is no greater
power than *belief*.
You can have all the skill in the
world but if you don't *believe*
you can do it, then what is the use
in the skill?'

Why You are Magnificent

step one – discover
chapter one

Oh darling, thank goodness you're here!

I have been waiting for you.

It's been a long time, too long really. Remember when you and I were so close when you were born. Remember those days when you used to kick your legs in the air, gurgled at anyone who would listen and dribbled to your heart's content. Those were the days!

Let's not leave it so long next time. In fact, let's make a promise that you and I stick together for the rest of time. Gosh, I've missed you.

Shine on, Sister!

Always,

Your Self-Esteem

'She knew she could, so she bloody well did!'

Famous quote amended by Me

I knew you would come! Congratulations, this is your first step to making you matter. I am delighted and privileged to have you on board and cannot wait to take you on an awe-inspiring journey. So, let's begin.

THE EARLY YEARS

All babies are born brimming with confidence with an expectation to be loved. Then slowly, life's experiences diminish this inner and outer shine. Have you ever noticed when you interact with a baby, they are often seen kicking their chunky legs, dribbling and gurgling as you coo over the buggy at them, and the baby smiles back, bright as a button without a care in the world. That baby isn't thinking 'Oooh, don't look at me, my legs are all dimply and I have tiny milk spots on my face.' What it is feeling and thinking is 'Hey you, look at me, I'm gorgeous!' You were born with an expectation to be loved and you were born to love, with an open heart and no judgement, just pure heartfelt confidence of who and what you are. You came in with a natural awareness and belief that you deserve to receive love while giving bundles of it too.

Did you know that the heart develops before the brain? In a human, the heartbeat begins around day 18 of development. Historically, the heart was thought to be the seat of thinking. The Egyptians believed that the heart was the source of the soul, the memory, emotions and personality. Aristotle said that the heart was the source of intelligence, motion and sensation, and the brain and lungs existed to cool the heart. It wasn't until the Renaissance that the Europeans decided that the heart functioned solely to pump blood. If you have been in love or even felt love for somebody or something, you feel it in your heart physically. It's not in the brain you feel love, it's in the heart and it's in the heart first.

I once read a quote about love: 'Your task is not to seek for love, but merely to seek and find all barriers within yourself that you have built against it.' We have built layers around our hearts to protect it, and in doing so have lost connection with our essence. Yes, things might have happened to us and from those things we have built barriers; it is this consequence that has hurt you and created the real disconnection. It's time to return to your heart, to love, and know that you deserve to be loved – after all, you are a being of love, just like that baby you once were, with love to give to others and yourself. Let's get back to basics and start again. You have lost yourself, your essence, and it's time to reclaim what is yours, your birthright – and that is love. Love of yourself. Love for others. And a love of life.

YOU'VE LOST THAT LOVING FEELIN

The Righteous Brothers were spot on with their 60s big hit. So many of you are existing feeling inadequate, as though you don't matter. Much of your value these days seem to come from how much you take care of others and put other people's needs before yours but it comes to the detriment of yourself. It seems these days that taking care of yourself emotionally, physically and spiritually, is a selfish concept. Well, time's up. The old paradigm isn't working anymore and society as a whole is exhausted, everyone is stressed, suffering from overwhelm and the state of the planet is simply mirroring our global consciousness. Now, you can't heal the whole planet but you can start with healing yourself.

Not only have you lost yourself and come away from the being of love, confidence and happiness that you are, but as a woman you have also forgotten who you are.

This book guides you back to your essence, opens up your mind and returns you to the real you, that being of love you are and always have been – you have simply forgotten.

CONFIDENCE

When I embarked on my journey of self-discovery, I would never have subscribed to the idea that I had low confidence or self-esteem. In all honesty, if anyone asked, I always described myself as being a confident person. As I look back at the beliefs I had formed as a child, I now understand that the choices and decisions I had made in later life were coming from a place of fear and lack: lack of confidence and true belief in myself and my abilities. My belief that I was a confident person was actually a belief in the mask that I wore to hide the fear and inadequacy that I really felt underneath but did a great job of hiding. So whether you think you have high, low or no confidence, every child has gone through some confidence-knocking moments at some point and these will have had some kind of effect on your adult choices and decisions at some stage.

Confidence is your birthright and underpins you as a person. It is about feeling sure of yourself and your abilities – i don't mean this in an arrogant way but in a secure and healthy way. If you have low confidence, it means you place little confidence or trust in yourself. When you lack confidence you stop taking care of yourself, you neglect your needs on every level, physically, mentally and emotionally. This is why confidence is so important; it is the foundation of you and your platform for growth through life.

Confidence is a belief in a skill and ability that you have. You can have low self-esteem but confidence in a skill that you have such as public speaking. You know that you can stand up on stage and give a good presentation, but when you step off, you're filled with 'Was I good enough? Did I say the right things? I looked ridiculous!' This is the fear of others' judgement because ultimately you don't believe in yourself. Did you know that one of the all-time greatest fears – greater than the fear of death! – is public speaking. Amazing to think that we hold people's judgement so high. Imagine if we let go of judgement by building our self-confidence so that when we stood up in front of others and did our best, this would be enough because you know in your heart that you are enough?

If your confidence has been bashed, battered and diminished, you need to return to the source of the pain and heal it so that you can grow and blossom as intended. Just like when a tree is struggling and withering, you give it the TLC it needs: water it, feed it, nourish it while pulling out the weeds that have accumulated beside it, the weeds that have been suffocating it. You find the root of the problem and pull it up. We will explore the root cause of your lack of confidence so that your self-esteem flourishes and, as a result, so will you.

SELF-ESTEEM

Self-esteem and self-confidence seem like the same thing, but they are not. Here is why. As I said, you might have no trouble at all standing in front of a big audience on stage, or a boardroom full of people and give a presentation or speech and work your magic, but at the same time, you feel rubbish about your ability to public speak – that opinion of you illustrates your lack of self-esteem. It's the way you view you. Self-esteem refers to how you feel about yourself overall, how much esteem, positive regard or self-love you have. Self-esteem develops from experiences and situations that have shaped how you view yourself today. Self-confidence is how you feel about your abilities and can vary from situation to situation. You may have healthy self-esteem, but low confidence about situations involving you and your sporting ability or artistic flair, for example. Although they are not the same, self-esteem and self-confidence go hand-in-hand. When you love yourself, your self-esteem improves, which makes you more confident. When you are confident in areas of your life, you begin to increase your overall sense of self-esteem. Feelings of 'not enough' and 'I don't matter' are linked with low self-esteem and it's important to understand the root of these feelings and thoughts so that you can move past them and return to your truth, the real you.

THE OPPOSITE OF LOVE IS FEAR

The consequence of low confidence and low self-esteem is life-shaping and life-changing. It determines the choices you make, as you are making them from a place of fear: fear that you will fail, fear that you will disappoint, fear that you may let others down, fear you might shame yourself, and the list goes on. When you are faced with that job opportunity and there is a niggling voice saying, 'You can't do that, you'll make a mess of it, you're too stupid.' That's your inner dialogue, making sure it's keeping you small. If you play small, play safe and dull your shine there is little chance of falling or failing. That is why so many people don't take risks in life because they are scared of the consequences. Are you prepared to let go of life and your potential just because your confidence has been shattered? As the late Wayne Dyer once said, 'Don't die with your music still inside you.' What if you healed that part of you so that you could shine, be your best version, fulfil your potential? How would that feel? Probably feels a bit scary at the moment but once you begin to explore your self-limiting beliefs and their origin, you can let them go. You can't heal something you don't understand.

Did you know that the feelings felt in the body when you are excited or in fear are the same? You can feel your heart pumping, maybe you're sweating, maybe your blood pressure and temperature are raised. Here is a great tool to use and one I used a lot. When you are in a state of fear or dread of something that you have to do, such as a presentation, as you feel the symptoms in your body, change the language you are using to dialogue with your mind and speak to your body as if you are excited. So, instead of saying 'I'm dreading this presentation, I can't wait for it to be over, I'm so nervous', change this to, 'I'm choosing to feel good about doing my presentation, I love doing these, they make me feel so empowered and confident.'

When you are in fear you produce the chemicals cortisol and adrenaline. However, when you are excited your body produces endorphins, serotonin, dopamine and oxytocin – a concoction of happy chemicals that make us feel good and are healthy chemicals. Too much of the fear-based chemicals can eventually have a detrimental effect on your health, so let's create less of the fight or flight in you and trick your mind with the words that you use.

Fear is the biggest goal-breaker there is. You create stories in your head based on your past and convince yourself that you are completely incapable of achieving your goals. Once you can understand the fear and beliefs around this, you can heal this and then get out of your own way. Fear dictates your choices and actions all through life, and you don't even realise it. You create fear! Believe it or not, fear is an illusion. It's not real. But what does that mean? Sounds bizarre, doesn't it!? You create scenarios in your mind, and then you feed off them. Fear is a reaction to a perceived threat – imagined or real. Once you understand where these fears came from you can simply move past them and achieve your goals. It really is that simple! Think about how many times you have put stories around a scenario that simply isn't true or you couldn't even know about. For example, when a friend lets you down, what is your inner dialogue during this scenario? Do you create a whole story around why they must be in a mood with you or avoiding you or do you simply accept that it is what it is and keep out of any stories? Or maybe you don't want to go to an event because the last time you did, you felt excluded by the hosts. What story are you telling yourself that is now stopping you going to what might be a productive and fun event, all because you have made a story up that the hosts don't like you or don't want you there when actually they are just preoccupied with their event? Truth is, it's just a story you're telling yourself and not real at all, and the story is keeping you from taking the leap or acknowledging a feeling you don't want to feel.

If there is something you are in fear of at the moment, perhaps taking the first steps on setting up a business, having another child, moving jobs, ending a relationship, ask yourself 'What is the worst that can happen if I did this?' When you come up with the answer, ask yourself 'And then what?' Keep going until you have exhausted the fear and come to the realisation that actually the story that you are telling yourself about the situation isn't that bad after all and is just one big story you are selling yourself to stop you moving forward. The inner conversation might go like this:

Your mind (in fear): I'm terrified of setting up a new business, I will probably fail, go bankrupt, lose my home, have nowhere to live and be left with nothing and everyone will judge me.

Me: What's the worst that will happen?

Adult you (reality): I lose money and fail.

Me: You learn some lessons and grow (the reframe). And then what?

You: I feel stupid and like a failure.

Me: You learn to let go of others' judgement (the reframe). And then what?

You: I get over it.

Me: You build strength to do it again with greater knowledge (the reframe). And then what?

You: I do it and succeed.

You see, your mind loves to put a big, fat story around things to stop you doing them in order to keep you safe, but this simple inner conversation takes you through the fear to a point where actually, there really isn't anything to fear other than your mind's chatter and judgement.

LITTLE YOU

Much of my work with clients and their self-esteem takes them back to their experiences in early childhood. You started life with confidence as a baby and had a healthy self-esteem but somewhere, somehow, sometime in your life this changed.

They needn't be big, traumatic events to knock your self-esteem off kilter. It could be a moment in the classroom when a teacher shamed you (even unintentionally), a critical word uttered by a parent or sibling that has stuck, a moment on the sports field when you made a mistake or even tripping over in public. When you look back, such little and seemingly meaningless things can have had a big impact on your confidence. Even if you feel there is no reason for being a bit out of sorts, just being in the modern world as a woman today can lead to this consciously and unconsciously. My experiences as a child were relatively uneventful on paper but the reality was I had a list of events that ultimately led to self-esteem failure.

I had a client who came to me with feelings of inadequacy and was suffering from chronic thrush that was affecting her sexual relationship and overall health. During our session together, it turned out these feelings of inadequacy were linked to various incidents in her early childhood, where she had experienced shame. When I prompted her mind to go back to events in her childhood, she went back to when she began her period at her school sports day. When she told her father, his response was extremely awkward and he didn't know how to handle it, quickly shutting her down to avoid the subject. This caused her to feel embarrassed and alone about something that was very natural. The next scene we went to was all to do with when she lost her virginity and the shame she felt when her friends asked her all about it. Again, there was that feeling of embarrassment despite this being another natural part of growing into a woman. The final scene was at her school where she was walking around in her sports kit with her father and some boys heckled her. Her father felt embarrassed and awkwardly ignored it, creating another episode of shame.

Following these relatively uneventful scenes (in terms of trauma), she had created beliefs that she had to hide her natural female traits and sexuality, that it wasn't safe to be a woman. These beliefs then resulted in chronic thrush which was her mind inhibiting her sexually and was like a barrier protecting her from exposing her sexual and female beauty.

Consciously, my client had no recollection of these events. However, once she was shown the link between her early childhood experiences and her current feelings of inadequacy, it was very clear to her how these beliefs had manifested in chronic thrush and low self-esteem.

This example shows you how the events in early childhood needn't be big or catastrophic events to create big feelings or emotions and, as a consequence, big reactions in the body on a physical level and in the mind emotionally.

THE SIMPLICITY OF CHILDREN

Children are naturally narcissistic. I mean this in the nicest possible sense! Up to a certain age, they are naturally selfish as a normal part of their development in which they work to get their needs met and can't understand other people's needs and desires because their main focus is their own needs and wants. With this in mind, when an adult displays a lack of love to you as a child or gives you little attention, fails to care for your needs, you turn this on yourself and make the situation about you. The reality is that your parent's mind is elsewhere, maybe because of stress, illness, or their own lack of self-worth. Instead, you have translated this treatment into beliefs such as, 'I'm not enough, I'm not lovable, I'm not worthy of love because if I was lovable enough, my parent would care for me.' It sounds quite simplistic when one breaks it down.

Up until the age of seven, children are working and functioning from their reptilian brain. Much of the brain chemistry and foundation of the brain make-up is formed during these formative years. There is the famous Aristotle saying, 'Give me a child until he is seven and I will show you the man'. A human's early experiences are so important as these are when the foundations are laid and we take them through to our adulthood. Therefore, we cannot ignore the early years in helping us to understand how and why we think a certain way and must go back to the early surroundings, environments, events and emotions that we experienced through these formative years. Children are simple and that's the beauty of them. Our early programming is formulated with these early experiences and if we don't look back to those moments, big or small, then we continue to run on this outdated programming. This is why so many people are walking talking adults living life with a child's perspective. Have you experienced moments in an adult relationship where you have felt like a child? Perhaps a boyfriend has let you down, neglected you because his mind has been elsewhere and instead of seeing that the situation was actually about him, meeting his needs and spending his time making himself feel enough through work or friendships, you have turned it on yourself and made it about you.

I had a client come to me because she was overwhelmed with life and wanted some help to get back to feeling herself. She felt sad and alone, with no spark. She was also struggling in her marriage with feelings of disconnection and lack of trust. During the session, we went back to when she was six years old and her father was leaving the family home for good, following the marriage break-up. Despite him saying to her that he loved her and he was sorry that he had to go, she felt abandoned, as if it was her fault; she felt alone, helpless and hopeless. The next scene we went to was when her parents were arguing and the father attempted to hit the mother. My client felt terrified and again those feelings of helplessness and hopelessness came up. When we explored her present feelings that she had come to me with, the link was clear between the feelings of powerlessness she had as a child and those same feelings as an adult.

She had created a belief that any man she loves will leave her, so she had created a marriage of distance (emotionally) to protect her from getting hurt as she had been as a little girl. She had made it her fault and made the scenario all about her, when it was never about her but about the parents separating because of their problems. As children, we can't see the bigger picture and we turn it on ourselves. She had never dealt with the sadness of the father leaving, she was still walking around feeling unloved, abandoned and alone. The reality was that none of the events that took place were about her but she had turned them on herself and created beliefs and stories around them that she had carried through until adulthood.

YOU ARE MAGNIFICENT

Being a female is the greatest blessing. Do you know how clever you are? You can make life; whether you choose to or not, you have the capability. On top of that, you can feed life; your body is designed to give food to your young. How clever are you?! Your womb is incredibly complex and magical, and sadly these days very misunderstood. Every single human being that has ever been alive upon this planet, now and throughout all of history, has achieved this existence thanks to this very organ. Now that's seriously something, isn't it? You and every person on Earth, now and before you, has been intimately acquainted with the uterus, since the dawn of your life, whether or not you have one personally within your own body. Women's bodies hold within them an incredible organ filled with sexual and creative power. It is time that you celebrated the astonishing capabilities and mysteries of the fantastic uterus and of women as a whole.

YOU ARE CYCLICAL

If you want to feel really good about yourself, let me share with you how amazing your body is. Did you know, a woman's menstrual cycles and stages of life are intrinsically linked to the cycles of the Earth, Moon and Sun. The moon cycle is 29.5 days, and the average woman's menstrual cycle is 29.5 days. Women whose cycles are closest to the 29.5-day cycle have higher rates of fertility. In addition, there are 13 moon cycles in a calendar year, and the average age of menarche (a girl's first menstruation) is age 13. The average age of menopause is 52, which is also the number of weeks in a year. There are an average of 4 weeks to a women's menstrual cycle and 4 seasons in a year. Women's ancient menstrual calendars consisting of notches carved into bone or stone are said to be some of the earliest forms of calendars known. Women's wombs hold a powerful connection to the astronomical cycles of the Earth, Sun and Moon. What?! Amazing, eh?!

HIT THE RESET BUTTON

You were born to shine but your light has been dulled and hidden at the cost of your confidence and self-esteem. How can you feel good about yourself when you are living in a society that is dumbing down your very essence? With the above in mind, how would it feel if you could rid yourself of the shame that is attached to the various parts of your cyclical life?

Let's start with the menarche, your first period. Until recently, and certainly through my school days, this was still quite awkward and particularly with boys! You couldn't go swimming, you couldn't play sport, you were 'on the blob'! Bloody hell! The reality is, at that point in a young lady's (maiden) life, you are making a massive transition from girl to creator, with the ability to create life and feed life. This transition should be wholly celebrated and respected. But it's not, and that's sad. However, you can change this. For every mum, auntie or friend reading this, let's empower the inner child within you, let them know they are okay, you can be proud of stepping in to your new phase and know that this is about empowering you, not shaming you any longer.

We must teach you and all those girls who later became leading ladies to honour that part of the month. The current patriarchal society is conditioning us to be more masculine, to push through the period pains, to work like a dog for every part of your 29.5-day cycle. But if you tuned into the different stages of your cycle, you would be far more creative, productive and useful. For example, when you are 'on' you really should be 'off'. It is a time of shedding, letting go and healing. A time for quiet contemplation, a 'period' to reflect on what you want to release that month, what emotions are now ready to be freed. In this time, you should slow down, take heed and nurture yourself much like you do in winter. But how does one do this when we have a job to hold down and a creative idea to bring to the table every working day? Of course, you can't just take a duvet day if and when you feel like it; this is about bringing an awareness to yourself and your body and being kinder with your words. It's a time to lower your expectations of yourself and to be compassionate to your needs. When you come out of this phase, having allowed nature to do what is needed, you come out more powerful, with bigger ideas, fresh to take on the challenges, ready to bloom just like in spring. I am evidence of this – the title and subtitle of this book, the preface, introduction and this very chapter were all written during this very stage! It came out of me with such ease because I had allowed myself to heal and let go, shed old stuff during my 'down time' and then the day after I was like a creative machine with creativity flowing out of me from every orifice!

Hands down, no BS, you are at your most creative at this time, you have the ability to come up with great ideas, lay down new concepts ready for the next phase of your cycle – the summer part. When you create and release an egg – the time when you are strong, can fulfil challenges and can take on pretty much anything (you know, that Wonder Woman feeling!?) – some of you might notice that you are more in touch with your sexual power and more horny even. This is the time in your cycle where you are at your most powerful, the opportunity of new life has been released and you are like an open flower showing the world how beautiful and magnificent you are. This is the time to push yourself and know that you have brilliant, creative capabilities at this time. It's okay to have great expectations of yourself because during this phase you are your own version of Wonder Woman.

But like all highs you must come down; post-summer you head into autumn, when you start to slow down, tune in and get ready for the winter (your period). Boy, if only you had known all of this earlier in life. You wouldn't be so hard on yourself, when you are trying to hit a deadline and muster up brilliant ideas every damn day! Well, now you can, and now you can teach your daughters, nieces, god-daughters and friends that you all hold the power, you are collectively amazing, you are cyclical, you are capable and it's time now to recognise the real power that lies within you and how you can harness it. And as you do your confidence will grow.

With this knowledge in hand, it's time to bring an awareness to each phase of your period so that you can respond to your needs, either slowing down or speeding up. When you can understand how your body is programmed, you can work with it rather than against it and balance your expectations depending on what part of your cycle you are in.

No wonder so many women in society are feeling 'not enough' and less than: your very essence has been shamed and shut down. You have been running on a lateral projection against your cyclical nature. There is a long way to go to heal the attitude towards women but if you alone understand how amazingly powerful and infinitely enough you are, you can lead by example and show other females around you what it is to be a walking talking symbol of 'enoughness' and confidence. It starts with you.

TAKE A WALK ON THE WILD SIDE

A woman is naturally wild, in the sense that she is in tune with nature, its seasons, the Earth, Mother Earth. When you return to you, you return to your wild self. I encourage you to return to that part of you, that natural and wild self that loves being by the sea, dancing bare foot, walking in nature, eating real, natural food, watching the stars and moon, allowing your hair to just be, natural, wild (when you can!) and going make-up free occasionally – believe me, it's liberating. Joy lies in the simple things in life: nature, love, family, friends. This is what feeds your soul, lights you up and brings you real happiness. It isn't about ticking boxes that society tells you to do or buy or have. Don't starve your soul any longer, this is about giving back to you and about real self-love. Get outdoors and embody the real woman in you. It's time to take a walk on your wild side; you were born to do it.

SELF-LOVE AND ALL THAT JAZZ

'Love is the great miracle cure. Loving
ourselves works miracles in our lives.'

~ Louise L. Hay.

A lot is written about self-love, you can barely pick up a magazine or self-help book without seeing something about it. Do you really know what it means and how to do it? And, most importantly, why you do it? First things first: when you have low or no self-esteem you also have low or no self-love. Self-love is a state of appreciation for yourself that grows from actions that support your physical, psychological and spiritual growth. If you're feeling low in self-confidence, one of the first things that goes is your level of self-love.

Self-love is dynamic; it grows as you carry out acts of self-love towards yourself. When you act in ways that grow self-love in you, you begin to accept your weaknesses, as well as your strengths, you no longer need to explain yourself when you trip up, you have compassion for yourself as a human being as you meander through life. That moment when you trip over in public is a prime example of how mean we can be to ourselves. The inner dialogue goes through the roof, you berate and shame yourself for 'looking silly, everyone saw me, I'm so useless'. Truth is, no one around paid much attention, and those that did felt compassion towards you and wondered if you were okay and felt your pain. A compassionate view to yourself would be to laugh or giggle, know that you are only human and sh*t happens and move on. Self-love is allowing you to fall flat on your face and still feel loved and supported by you, not shamed or judged.

Currently in society there is a notion that if you self-love and take care of yourself, it's selfish.

As a woman, you are (regrettably) conditioned to put others' needs before yours, because you are programmed to be a giver and caretaker of everyone but yourself. Do you do this? Are you one of the many who think self-love is just another act of self-indulgence and an unnecessary act of self-gratification? Do you feel that others might judge you if you allocate time for yourself? Do you feel you're meant to suffer and life is meant to be hard?

Self-love was a completely new concept to me; five years ago, I had no idea what it was. It turns out that the reason I didn't know what it was is because I have pretty much never done it. I had to learn to love me, not just on the outside but, more importantly, on the inside. This had been a conscious daily practice of talking to myself kindly, being compassionate to myself during challenging times and learning how to put my needs ahead of other people's. It took time and practice and at times it still catches me out and I hear the negative voice creep in; but it's not long before I notice it and return to a place of love and compassion towards myself. For me, self-love hasn't just been about the way I talk to myself but also the way I feed myself, exercise my body, the amount I do (or rather don't) put in my diary, and the choices I have made regarding the environment I choose to be in socially and physically (in nature as much as possible). Self-love is a way of life, it's my overall code of conduct and I ensure these days that every choice I make and action I take is from a place of self-love. So if you're reading this and thinking, 'oh hell, I have never self-loved, ever', fear not. You can learn to do this, just like I did. Start by making you the priority as of today and begin by slowly introducing self-love into your daily life and eventually it will become your way of life.

First, let me get clear on how I see self-love. I like to think of self-love as the umbrella term, under which there is self-acceptance, self-compassion and self-care. One cannot exist without the others if you are seeking to be in self-love. They co-exist and when you practise all parts you are officially practising self-love. Then I hear you ask, what do I mean by self-acceptance, self-compassion and self-care? Let me explain:

☆ **Self-compassion is** about being kind to yourself. Using that tender and nurturing voice to support, help and heal your inner emotional turmoil.

☆ **Self-acceptance is** accepting you as you are without judgement. You're not good, bad, right, wrong, fat, thin, pretty or ugly. You just are and that is just right. People talk about 'loving ourselves' and I believe that is a big expectation, especially since most of us have come from a place of self-loathing and self-esteem collapse. Self-acceptance is a much more achievable and realistic goal.

☆ **Self-care is** the act of self-love. It isn't just taking a warm bath and getting your nails done. It is saying 'no' to commitments when your week is already jam packed. It is cancelling or postponing arrangements if it is better for your emotional, physical and spiritual well-being. It is speaking your truth while setting boundaries (personal guidelines or limits on how you wish to be treated) with others from a place of love and compassion.

Sadly for most, none of these come naturally and you need to learn how to accept yourself, learn how to talk to yourself with compassion and how to take care of yourself. There is no handbook to life. You have your parents as role models but, let's be honest, they muddled through too.

On Valentine's Day, you buy for your loved one, you dress up, you put your lippy on, make them or take them for a lovely meal. Yet when it comes to doing the same for you, you feel guilt or shamed for allocating time for yourself. Whose critical voice is in your head telling you it's selfish to take care of yourself?

The bottom line is, it is an investment to self-love. Without it, your emotional, physical and spiritual side suffers and so do those around us. If you aren't keeping your mind and body healthy and clear then it impacts the relationships around you. And bitterness starts to seep in to all areas creating disharmony and disease. Did you know that the origin of the word disease comes from a French term meaning 'lack of ease'? When lack of harmony and flow occurs in your body, so does a sense of dis-ease, disease.

It's selfish not to self-love. Make self-love a priority. From today, even a little act towards that goal will grow that dynamic part of you, and gradually your self-confidence and self-esteem will flourish. When you give yourself self-love, you nourish and nurture your mind, body and soul giving yourself time to heal physically, emotionally and spiritually. When you self-love, you show yourself unconditional love and understanding while meeting your needs, needs that weren't met by your parents or early caregivers as a child. Whatever love you didn't receive as a child and whatever needs weren't met back then, it's okay because your adult self has just shown up and is ready to make you matter, make you feel loved and meet your needs. Welcome her, thank her for being here, for showing up finally. You've been waiting a long time and finally the wait is over. Time to make you truly matter, time to make you whole.

Start with this simple exercise:

☆ *Every day, write down five things that you are proud of, no matter how big or how small – They all count.*

RE-PAIRING YOU

Let's now begin your reconnection to self. We do this by meeting your inner child, that little girl that lives within you and holds all your past emotional memories. I will explain and explore the inner child connection later on in the book but as a starter, one way that I encourage my clients to connect with themselves is to bring a photo of their younger selves to the session and we explore her qualities, feel the energy she is radiating, feel the freedom she felt before all the self-limiting beliefs kicked in. Before I do this, I ask my client to tell me the kind of things they say to their adult self. I then hold up their younger photo and ask them if they would say those things to their little version. This always evokes a reaction of sadness and a big realisation of just how mean that inner critic has been to the adult self and, consequently, to the internal little self; just because she is now an adult, she doesn't deserve that. I always get my client to put that photo up of her at home so that they can stay connected and remember what words that little girl needs to hear, like she is loved unconditionally, safe, protected, enough just as she is. It's all about re-parenting your younger self and nourishing yourself where you were once malnourished with love, compassion and care.

I encourage you to do the same. This is your first step to uncovering the pain, sadness and self-limiting beliefs that you have stored inside you for way too long. This might be hard at first; it takes courage to admit openly how you have been talking to yourself but it's okay. If this brings up any emotions that you feel are too painful or hard to handle, please seek the advice of a friend or family member to talk through what is coming up for you, or if necessary book in with a trained therapist. If it brings on tears, please don't judge this. I always tell my clients that tears are a healthy way to release stuck old emotions. I love the saying 'my tears watered my soul and gave me strength to bloom'. When we cry, we are releasing emotions and feelings that we have stuffed down and buried deep inside our bodies in order to avoid feeling them. Rest assured, this is old energy that has been pushed deep down inside for far too long and it's time to let it go so that you can make space for your dreams. When we suppress emotions, we don't just block out the negative ones, we block out the positive ones too; so when we finally let go of old negative emotions, we make space for more love and joy. What a treat.

I want you now to take some time to feel the energy of the little you. See her in your mind's eye. Sit for a moment, with your feet on the ground. Breathe in, allowing your energy to drop down your body, feeling your feet on the ground and bottom on the seat. Take a moment to read the visualisation *Upgrading the Child*[1] below and follow the instructions:

---

[1]   Copyright Marisa Peer

☆ *Close your eyes and take in three deep breaths. Now visualise the home you lived in as a child, see the detail on the front door, notice the sounds and smells around you. Open the front door, notice the pictures on the wall, the smell. Is it warm or cold? Is there noise or is it silent? Now go to the bedroom you had there. As you get to the door, it is closed; notice the detail on the door. Behind that door is a little version of you. She holds all the feelings and memories that you had as a child. Go over to her and sit down next to her, this is your inner child – your emotional self. Breathe in. Smile and connect with her, notice what she is doing and how she is feeling. Hold her hand and let her know you are here for her now and looking forward to reconnecting with her after all this time so you can repair her self-esteem together. I want you to ask her how she is feeling, really get her to open up and share what's bothering her and what's stopping her from creating her dream life. Allow her to speak, the chances are she has felt shut down and not heard. Take as long as you need to dialogue with her. Tell her you are sorry that she feels the way she does and things are going to change from today. If any of this brings on tears, please allow them to flow, I suspect they are tears of relief, realisation and the start of your return to a confident self. When you are ready, taking as much time as you need, slowly open up your eyes.*

When you are ready, answer these questions, writing down the first things that come to your mind:

☆ *How old is she?*

☆ *How is she feeling*

☆ *What is stopping her from achieving her dreams?*

You can revisit this bedroom at any time when you need answers about what is stopping you move forward. She holds the answers to all your current states of mind. If another age child comes forward then this is the one that has come forward for healing.

Inner child work is a huge part of what I do with my clients, it has been the foundation of my healing and continues to be the go-to for my own growth. I talk more about this later in the book but believe me this is fundamental in your transformation as we grow you back up.

With the focus of this book being about reclaiming your confidence so that you can shine just like you were born to, let's focus our attention a little bit more on you and helping you to shine bright. To do this, I'm going to put you in the spotlight. The term 'in the spotlight' means to project a spot of light in order to brilliantly illuminate a person. Let's begin to illuminate you, you brilliant person.

☆ IN THE SPOTLIGHT ☆
MEETING YOUR LITTLE ONE

Now I want you to tune in to your adult self and the negative self-talk that you use. Imagine a challenging time when you are struggling to do something or be something. Get your journal and list the sorts of things you say to yourself during these times:

These might be something like 'you're so stupid, you can't do that', 'you can't wear that, you look too old', or something like 'you can never get a partner, no one will love you like you are'.

Whatever comes to mind. This will be hard to write down and might shock you at first but just go with it, allow whatever to come up and write it all down. Keep going, even when you think there is nothing else to write. Keep exploring times when you have been hard on yourself, when you think you have failed or disappointed yourself or other people.

Find a photo of you that corresponds in age to the inner child that you met in the visualisation. I want you to look at her, remembering all the things that you have said to yourself as an adult. You have been saying these things to her too. I know, it's hard, so hard to hear this but rest assured this is your path to healing you both. This is the beginning of something very special. As you look at the photo, tell her how sorry you are for the words that you have used and make a pact with her that you are going to work together to heal this part of you. As you look at the photo, I want you to write down all the qualities this little version of you possesses. Again, even when you think you have finished, write more.

I want you to put this photo up at home, on your phone, on your fridge, on the mirror as you brush your teeth, and every time you look at the photos, remember just how special this little girl is. This little girl is you. You have all those qualities within you; some of them have been forgotten or buried and you are going to reactivate that part of you and bring her back to life. Whenever you catch sight of this image, I want you to tell her how much you love her and how much you believe in her. Tell her how you love her unconditionally, remind her it is safe to be her, tell her you will listen to her now, that she is safe, loved and, of course, completely enough.

Now I want you to transfer the above qualities that you have written down about your inner child and write them about you, starting with the words I AM; she is you and you are her.

Once you have done this you are going to see clearly how you have been mistreating yourself and the need for a massive dose of self-love. I'm going to write you a prescription now. The best way to take it is every day, little-by-little, until the symptoms reduce and eventually vanish. Just like antibiotics, you have to keep taking it, even when you think the symptoms have subsided, to ensure you have a lasting cure. Here is my list of acts of self-love: choose which ones resonate with you and repeat them every single day. It is really important to build this into your routine. There might be weeks where you fall out of the habit but when you bring some awareness to it, you will realise that you haven't been taking care of yourself as you should and need to reset your focus. Compassion extends to when you break a habit, this is the time you need it most.

Remember, when you self-love you are making your emotional, physical and spiritual self the priority.

SELF-LOVE COMES IN MANY FORMS

☆ *Choose yourself* – Even if it means upsetting others (that's their stuff) and not being popular anymore. Even if it means leaving a party before anyone else because you feel tired, overwhelmed, or just plain feel done with the crowd. As long as you explain from a loving and compassionate place, you are ensuring your matters matter.

☆ *Praise yourself* – Compliment the things that you do well and give yourself compassion for what you have found challenging. Write them down, keep a note.

☆ *Love every part of you* – Love yourself inside and outside. No one remembers a good-looking b*tch, they remember a beautiful soul.

☆ *Do what lights you up* – Whether that is taking an Epsom salt bath, being with friends and family, walking in nature, buying yourself flowers or reading a book, just do it. When you do what you love, it sets your soul alight.

☆ *Speak your truth* – Unsaid words harm us, close your throat and make us feel like you are betraying yourself as you aren't talking from your heart about what you believe in.

☆ *Spend time with you* – When you connect with you, you can never be lonely again. You are your greatest friend. Enjoying your company is a gift.

☆ *Nurture your body* – Speak kindly to it, rest it, love it and exercise it.

☆ *Honour your gut instinct* – It is always right. Go with what you know in your heart and not your head.

☆ *Let mistakes go* – You are human, we make mistakes. They are our best teachers, let them go and learn from them. Use compassion in the face of them but never berate yourself for making them.

☆ *Dream big* – And while you do it, believe in yourself. You deserve success and you can manifest your dreams. Don't allow other people's limitations to be your limitations.

☆ *Use kind words to yourself and others* – The words you use are linked to your emotional and physical health. Choose kind ones always.

☆ *Wear clothes that make you feel good* – Clothes that express you and your individuality.

☆ *Build a life that you love* – Don't wait for Mister Right thinking that he will solve all your problems. Make a life that you love and are happy in and then your life partner will arrive.

☆ *Stay away from gossip* – Don't be drawn in to other people's gossip, this is just another way to judge, and when you judge others, you are judging yourself. You deserve better.

☆ *Lovingly accept yourself for who you are* – You are perfectly imperfect and that is just right.

☆ *Validate yourself* – As long as you are happy with you, then the validation of others is irrelevant.

☆ *Be in nature* – Nature heals, you are a natural being and when you spend time with Mother Nature you reconnect with yourself.

☆ *Have pyjamas days* – These are the best. It's okay to binge watch your favourite show if it nurtures your soul.

☆ *Do yoga* – This releases blocks in your physical and emotional body and resets your mind.

☆ *Meditate, meditate, meditate* – Your mind is the holder of all your thoughts, when you meditate you are able to connect with yourself on your deepest level.

☆ *Accept yourself* – Every single part of you even your dark side; it's there for a reason, acknowledge her and greet every part of you with open arms.

☆ *Live a life aligned with your values* – Meet your needs, instead of putting everyone else's ahead of yours.

☆ *Follow your soul's calling* – This is the biggest form of self-love you can perform. When you are aligned with your purpose, you fulfil your soul's calling, your heart's desire.

SELF-LOVE STARTS TODAY

Build these acts of self-love into your routine starting from today. It takes practice to say 'no' and to meet your needs, as it doesn't come naturally to you but the more you do it, the more you build the mind muscles and new habits are formed.

SELF-BELIEF

'The strongest factor for success is self-esteem, believing you can do it, believing you deserve it and believing you will get it.'

–Anonymous

I talked about the difference between self-confidence (the belief in a skill or an ability that you have) and self-esteem (the way you view yourself). Now I'm going to explore the importance of self-belief. The difference between self-esteem and self-belief is simple. Self-esteem as you know is the way you view yourself as a whole, self-belief is a positive mental attitude towards yourself and your abilities. While having self-belief, it is also important to have self-awareness in order to have a realistic belief in yourself. There is no point having belief in the ability to sing and get a record deal if, truth be known, you can't sing a single note – you've seen it many times on X Factor. Having a balanced, realistic and positive state of mind about your capabilities is self-belief.

There is no greater power than belief. You can have all the skill in the world but if you don't believe you can do it, then what use is the skill? As you build your self-esteem, you need to build your self-belief. They go hand-in-hand if you want to achieve success. Many of you lack self-belief because you have never taken the time to truly explore your strengths or even your goals. You are expected to be good at everything. At school, you are expected to get A* in all subjects, but this is unrealistic. We are all gifted in our own special way but you cannot be expected to be proficient at everything; if we were, we would all be robots. You are the very opposite of this: you are unique, there is only one of you on this whole planet. Lack of self-belief slowly creeps in when you are attempting to shine at everything. As Albert Einstein once said, 'Everybody is a genius but if you judge a fish by its ability to climb a tree, it will live its whole life believing that it is stupid.' Focus on your strengths and once you establish those you can achieve your goals and develop your self-belief.

Take time to think about what your strengths are, write them down in your journal. Take time to look over them and think about where you are using them in your career or life. Are you using them or letting them go to waste? Are you struggling with a job where you're doing something that doesn't come naturally to you? Focus on your strengths, it's where your passion lies. Harness and develop them, become the master of your strengths. Who wants to be mediocre at something you don't really like and isn't your passion. When you embrace a life or career that you're good at, you will naturally excel at it and in return, build your confidence, self-belief and self-esteem and, ultimately, build a life you love.

When you are comfortable with exploring your strengths, think about what it is you would like to achieve? What do you need in order to achieve them and what is stopping you achieving them. You already know some of your answers: lack of self-confidence and self-esteem, coupled with fear of failure. But how about understanding what it is you want from life and what it requires from you? All too often, you focus on what you aren't good at which feeds the feelings of inadequacy. What you focus on becomes the driving force, so let's change the focus. When you hold beliefs like 'I am a failure', you make subconscious choices that validate your feelings.

I had a client reach out for help as she was struggling with motivation and feelings of inadequacy. She wanted to publish her novel but was finding it difficult to motivate herself and was struggling at every setback that unfolded. She was starting to believe her novel wasn't good enough and that, ultimately, she wasn't good enough.

During our session, she went back to when she was five years old and loved drawing. She showed her father the drawing, which she was very proud of, and he responded with 'you can do better than that', leaving her feeling hurt and very disappointed. The next scene she went to was at school when her teacher was asking the class some questions. She was confident she knew the answer so she stood up in front of the class and gave her answer, which turned out to be incorrect. The teacher shamed her in front of the class and she sat feeling very embarrassed and ashamed of herself particularly as she thought she knew the answer. The final scene was when she was 18 and she failed her English A-level, despite thinking she would breeze through it having done lots of work ahead of the exam. When she received the result she was devastated, bereft and felt ashamed because she had always thought she was good at English.

She had created a belief that everything she thinks she is good at, it turns out she isn't, and that she is therefore inadequate and not enough. She was now projecting this belief onto her novel and it was leading to a lack of motivation, feelings of failure and an overwhelming feeling of inadequacy. Once she could see how this early belief was affecting her adult perspective, she could rewire her way of thinking. The reality was, she was a very talented author and when I asked her before the session whether or not her book was any good, she said 'Yes, I believe it is' but her subconscious programming was trickling through to her present reality. Despite her having the skills, her lack of belief in herself was hindering her progress.

☆ IN THE SPOTLIGHT ☆
STRENGTHS AND GOALS

When you explore your strengths and goals, I want you to go on a journey and really dig deep in to your mind and bring forward all the tools, abilities and characteristics that illustrate your strengths. Go back to times in your life when you achieved something that you were proud of and figure out what traits assisted you in achieving that goal. When people compliment you, what type of things do they say to you?

Keep going until you have exhausted all areas of your past and racked every part of your brain; you must list a minimum of 25 strengths. Really allow yourself to uncover strengths that you had forgotten you have. There is no right or wrong, good or bad, just let yourself flow and feel free to add more to your list.

If you notice resistance, simply thank that part of your mind but instruct it that you are choosing to focus on your strengths, and say out loud, 'I have many strengths and I am choosing to honour them now.'

Here are a few suggestions to start with that might jog your memory and get your mind flowing with ideas: Good with people, creative with words, problem solver, funny, kind, compassionate, organised, reactive, calm.

Congratulations! Look at how many strengths you have and some of them I bet you didn't even know you had. I want you to put this piece of paper up on your wall and remember just how many strengths you have! Now I want you to dig a little deeper. You have listed the strengths that you think you have – now let's ask some other people in your life.

☆ IN THE SPOTLIGHT ☆
BUDDY EXPLORATION

I want you to choose three people, family or friends, and ask them to list five of your strengths. Allow them to come to their own conclusions and don't talk them out of any even if you disagree. Once you have completed this exercise, you will find that you have at least 30, maybe even as much as 40 or more strengths that you hadn't acknowledged and probably give little thought to.

Turn this into one big mind map with 'my strengths' as the central idea/words in the middle of your piece of paper and then have all your strengths branching off from the centre. When it is complete, you can use this as a confidence booster when you are feeling stuck or lacking motivation because you feel you aren't good at anything. When your internal dialogue is saying one thing, remind it why it is incorrect and that you are full of strengths. You can use it later on, when you discover what your goals, to ensure that your goals align with your strengths – no use wanting to be a fishmonger if you hate fish or anything to do with the sea! Then go back to your goals and refocus ensuring that you're using your strengths and in a job or career that plays to your unique cocktail of strengths.

BACK OF THE NET!

Goals matter and you need to get clear what yours are. I have, over the last few years, put my goals down on a vision board. Last year's one had a rough book title and cover, hosting a women's event and public speaking. With those ticked off, this year's looks like this: Online business, online course and hosting retreats.

I want you to list your goals, focusing on what you would like to achieve if you had high self-esteem. For example, what is calling you? What would you love to achieve if there were no limits or financial constraints? Or no fears? If you close your eyes right now and ask yourself what you would like to achieve in the next 5 years, what comes to mind? Just let yourself write and keep out of judging. Maybe it's quitting your job and fulfilling your heart's desire, setting up a business, spreading your message, becoming more creative and making a business of it. Or maybe it's riding a horse, learning a new hobby or clearing out the house.

Then I want you to answer these simple questions:

☆ *What is stopping you from achieving your goals?*

☆ *What do you need to heal in order to achieve your goals?*

☆ *What goal would you most like to achieve from your list?*

'Nothing is impossible.
The word itself says I'm possible'

– Audrey Hepburn

VALIDATION IS ALL YOU NEED

Too often people seek validation from people around them and think that if others believe in you that is all you need. But it's quite the contrary. Of course, as children you got your validation and self-worth initially from your parents and key caregivers and as you grew, their words and their belief in you became your foundation of belief in yourself. If there was little support and encouragement as a child, it's likely that you aren't your number one cheerleader.

The good news is we can rewrite this part of our life. We can recreate a new foundation of belief, encouragement and support for everything we do, big or small. And when we make mistakes, we use kind and compassionate language reminding ourselves there are no mistakes, only lessons and growth. It starts with you and your belief in you, it doesn't matter how much your friends or family believe in you or not, it's your self-belief that propels you to achieve and succeed.

VALUES

Another very important area you must explore is your values. Until my journey of discovery, I didn't know what this meant, but once I did, it was an incredibly powerful tool to helping me understand what drives me. When you can understand your values, you can make choices and decisions based on what is important to you. It is widely acknowledged that individuals experience greater fulfilment when they live by their values. However, if you fail to live by your values, your mental, emotional and physical state suffers.

☆ IN THE SPOTLIGHT ☆
WHAT ARE YOUR VALUES?

When you explore your values, you are simply working out what is important to you. When I detailed my values, they looked like this: my primary ones were love, family and security. You can see from the nature of them, they are linked to my past and what I believed I didn't receive as a child but is now a priority and a high value of mine. I felt unlovable as a child therefore it is important to me to be surrounded by love and to give love. At times as a child I didn't feel happy in the family dynamic, so it was important to me to create a happy family. Finally, as I often felt fearful, it is important to me to feel safe and secure. Other values of mine that I would call secondary are honesty, trust, communication, fun, being included and being heard. Now explore your primary and secondary values.

What are your values, what is important to you? List them and become familiar with what is important to you. Is it freedom, financial abundance, autonomy, love, family, security, growth, honesty? As you list them put them in order of importance. You might need to play with the order a few times to really ensure they are listed in the correct order.

When you can align your strengths, goals and values, you can get a very clear picture of what you want to do, why you want to do it and how it looks and feels. This gives a foundation to work towards as you build your confidence and move towards creating the life you want in Step 3, when you will explore your goals further. But first, you must detox your emotions.

NO THANKS, THERAPY ISN'T FOR ME

With a hand on my heart, I never believed I would have needed therapy and someone to 'fix' me and put me back together, but I did. Once I admitted I needed help and that life was too tricky to handle, that I was worn out and limping through life, I felt liberated. So many of us are walking around unconscious but consciously making a decision to be unconscious. I like to call it conscious dissonance: you know that fizzy drinks are bad for you and that they cause cancer and rot your brain but you just keeping drinking them. It's that Diet Coke break kind of moment you can't let go of even though you know you should. Well, it's the same with your self-limiting beliefs. They are the things that are stopping you achieving your heart's desire. You know that you often treat yourself unkindly and punish yourself with your words but you can't seem to let go of the behaviour and get out of your own way. You know you need to look at your fears and where they came from but you can't face the music.

When I turned up on my coach's door, the wonderful Michelle Zelli (now friend and mentor) one sunny August day, I felt the same. I was full of fear but I knew life couldn't go on as it was. I had to face my shadows in order to move forward, to keep my husband, be a good mum and to stay sane. I sat in the therapy chair, petrified, wondering what the heck she was going to tell me. Was I resentful because life is meant to be like this? Well, in my case, I discovered I loved drama and would always create a dramatic or stressful situation and those fearful questions I was asking myself were another dramatic story I was telling myself. My voice in my head was diabolical: 'you're so stupid, what's wrong with you, you don't matter'. Something had to give. If I was going to get something out of life and let go of my out-of-control mind then I needed to step up and understand why I was like I was. And so do you. I remember that day vividly. Michelle Zelli asked me 'Where do you see yourself in the family dynamic?' I curled my lip up and said, 'Dunno, fairly insignificant.' I didn't think anything of it at the time but that feeling and label was defining me.

As humans, we are programmed to move away from pain and towards pleasure.[2] It happened to be the case that the present feelings that I was having were pain and the alternative (of releasing what was in my way) was pleasure despite it being painful to do. In truth, the letting go was less painful than how I felt. Holding on to the present feelings wasn't an option. I had to be honest with myself. I had to admit that certain things in life had hurt me and as a response I had built a structure around me, my heart and my vulnerability. I see it like an onion in the middle of which is our essence, our truth, our purity and an open heart. But as life unfolds, we cover it with layer after layer of skin until we are far from our essence or core. When you cut into an onion, you can see the layers, perfectly formed. Slowly you must peel away the layers in order to return to yourself, your truth. I had to be brave. No one said it would be easy to admit that my Mum and Dad were physically and emotionally absent when I was young and that I had ended up with little or no self-worth. I had created, as Michelle would say, a Disney story around my childhood, you know, with rose-tinted glasses. It took courage to confront and admit that actually I felt very alone, abandoned and lost as a child and as a consequence internalised a lot of my feelings. Admitting this was the best decision I have ever made and it has set me free to return to myself and achieve what I dreamt of before I got self-limiting beliefs. This book is a symbol of how far I have come. You

---

[2] Copyright Marisa Peer

owe it to yourself to face the music, show up, look your fears straight in the eyes and say, 'I'm here and I'm ready to make me matter so that I can live the life I was destined to live because I deserve it.' Make that your mantra, say it loud, say it proud!

'I'm here and I'm ready to make me matter so that I can live the life I was destined to live because I deserve it.'

I went to a wedding recently where I hadn't seen most of the guests since school when I was 18. When I shared that I was a coach and explained that I ended up doing it following my own personal breakdown and subsequent journey, one by one people admitted to me that they had had a similar road block. By the end of the wedding, and as I reflected on the wonderful day, I chuckled to myself; all but about one person had been through therapy one way or another. I was like everyone, after all, they just chose to keep it to themselves until I shared my story. You're not on your own and it's okay to admit that you need a helping hand with life – there is no text book or idiot's guide to life. So let's put the stigma of therapy to bed once and for all and let's get stuck in. The only way is up, after all. This is simply about having a coach, a mentor or whatever you want to call it, to help you see your blind spots so that you can move forward. I'm honoured to be your guide. Let's do this.

What have I discovered?

What do I want to change?

What do I want to create?

☆

'Leave a little *glitter*
everywhere you go'

Road Blocks to Your Magnificence

chapter two

Darling,

Let me take you by the hand so you can let go of those old stories you've been telling yourself. It's all an illusion because the truth is, you are amazing; you just forgot how to be you, the real you. Off with the mask, out with the roles that kept you small. You have a gift just waiting to be unleashed.

We make an awesome team, let's do this!

Shine on, Sister!

Always,

Your Self-Esteem

'She wasn't a princess who needed saving, she was a god-damn Superwoman who has got her shit handled.'

An anonymous quote reinterpreted by Me

We did some early exploration of your self-limiting beliefs in the first chapter when you connected with your inner child. It can be hard to acknowledge, and even believe for that matter, that that was really how you felt. I bet there were moments where you shut the feelings and thoughts down because they were too painful to visit and acknowledge. This is where you have to be brave and put on your courageous pants and really look in the face of your old programming – this way you can change it. This chapter is all about the discovery of our beliefs so that we can change them and then create a life we love.

As you journey through this book, you will learn stuff about yourself that you may or may not like, that may surprise you or even shock you. I want you to remember, that your subconscious mind will only bring forward what you are ready to process and heal. At times it might feel painful but in other moments you might feel liberated from knowing and understanding that you're not alone and that others feel just like you. Remember to always look on with a sense of curiosity and without judgement. Keep an open mind, remind yourself of your intention before you began this book and keep going back to this. When you have an open and curious mind, the world is your oyster, my darling. I can't stress to you the importance of sitting back and being an observer of your thoughts and emotions. Allow them to come up, let the energy rise like bubbles from your heart, breathe and then let them go. When people talk about enlightened beings, they are those who are unattached and simply observe the melodrama and mind chatter that plays out in our head. You are not your thoughts, you are not your emotions, you are the observer of them. You are the master of your mind, not the other way. Sit back, observe, breathe and let it go. It really is that simple, only it takes a lifetime of dedication and practice but the reward is real freedom and even enlightenment. Light me up baby!

SHAME IS NOT ON YOU!

In the previous chapter, you discovered some of your limiting beliefs and got an insight into how you felt as a child, something you might not have ever known before. It's a big moment of illumination and for many can be difficult to compute because shame is there on your shoulder telling you that it's not okay to feel this, admit this or even know this – it's best left alone and buried. Well, that's an old school of thought, we are not the generation that puts on a stiff upper lip and shuts down our feelings. It's okay to admit that you have experienced moments and times of hardship. It's okay to say that your mum and dad didn't meet your needs. It's okay to honour your emotions, not shame them. We must allow our feelings and thoughts to arise without judgement, with only a curious eye, otherwise we end up shutting them down and not healing them. The bold truth is, if we don't heal them when they come up for healing, then they will come back around and bite you on the arse!

Shame is such a big part of women's lives these days. We are shamed about feeling, shamed about being a woman, shamed for having our periods or being premenstrual, we feel shame for aging, or being perimenopausal, shamed for showing our emotions, shamed for being ourselves or talking our truth and the list goes on. It's everywhere and it cannot be ignored.

What is shame exactly? Shame is essentially there to alert us to when we have acted out of our value system. For example, when we have got really drunk, danced on tables, fallen off tables, broken a heel and then snogged the bar tender, and woken up with little memory. Shame is the moment you ask your flatmate for the real truth, 'What happened last night, was I a mess?' Fingers crossed they reply with a positive recollection. However, if they go on to recall all the details, what you feel as she reminisces about the evening and its events is a feeling of shame. Because the truth is, if alcohol had not been involved, you wouldn't have acted outside of your value system.

You may sometimes confuse shame with feelings of guilt. Here's why:

☆ When you feel shame, you're feeling that *your whole self* is wrong.

☆ When you feel guilt, you're making a judgement that *something you've done* is wrong.

Shame goes even deeper than this. It is a powerful emotion that can cause people to feel defective, unacceptable, even damaged beyond repair. I have had clients come to me with feelings of deep shame for even existing, shame for being born, shame of being themselves.

Did you know that shame is only felt by humans? No other living thing experiences feelings of shame, it is purely a human creation and made up of the stories we tell ourselves about us. Shame keeps us, and others, small. Shame is the feeling you feel when you trip over in public and those feelings and array of thoughts about how embarrassed you are because your whole self is stupid, worthless, ridiculous – none of it of course is true, it's just the shame-based story you have told yourself based on outdated beliefs.

Most emotions we feel come and go and are met with fleeting thoughts at the time. But shame is different and those who experience shame are shame-based thinkers. They constantly look for the 'defective' storyline in day-to-day life and feel an overall sense of 'I'm not right, I'm defective, incompetent, unwanted, bad' and have a constant awareness of one's defects. I believe that women in today's society feel this deep down and we need to repair this. I have shown you the power of being a woman and the gifts that come with this; we must honour these gifts and recognise on a daily basis that we are worthy and valued. The current patriarchal model may not be ready to accept this concept wholeheartedly just yet but things are changing and shifts are taking place. It's up to you to let go of shaming yourself, your feelings, your overall sense of being. Enough of the shaming, belittling and putting down of others too. This goes for feelings also, allow yourself to feel and allow others too. All too often we feel a certain way and we shame ourselves, which leads to judgement of the feeling and then shutting down.

The aim is to get to a point where we honour the feelings coming up, observe them and allow them to come forward. So when you did the exercise earlier of connecting with your self-limiting beliefs and didn't want to acknowledge some, it's because you went into shame and judgement of them. First, let me tell you sister, it's okay to feel, you are allowed to feel however you want. Let me go a bit deeper into emotions and what they are.

WEIRD SCIENCE

Before I go any further, I want to talk to you briefly about vibration and the small matter of 'everything is energy'. This is a massive part of Step 3 when we open you up to the powers of the Universe. But before we get to that I wanted to share with you the fundamentals on this subject so that you can grasp an early understanding of how emotions affect you.

So here goes, EVERYTHING IS VIBRATING. Everything. Like I mean, everything! If you don't know about the findings of Einstein then this is your mini science lesson on a matter that will shift your perspective on everything. This is the Law of Vibration – don't be mistaken, this isn't the Law of Attraction, we'll get on to that later but this law serves as the foundation for the Law of Attraction. The Law of Vibration states that every single thing in the whole entire Universe moves and vibrates – everything is vibrating at one speed or another. Nothing rests. Nothing. Everything you see around you is vibrating at one frequency or another, and so are you. But the key is, your frequency is different from other things in the Universe and that's why it seems like you are separated from what you see around you such as people, animals, plants, trees and furniture.

With this in mind, our bodies vibrate at a certain frequency. A healthy body, for example, would be resonating on a high vibration frequency and would vibrate at approximately 72–90 MHz, while an unhealthy body and one with disease begins at a vibration of 58 MHz; and as the diseases become more severe, such a cancer, the body might be vibrating at 42MHz. You may be wondering why on earth I'm telling you this. Well, it's simple. As I said everything we see has a frequency. It's not just things that we see – thoughts and feelings also have their own vibration. The more negative the thought or feeling, the lower the vibration. As these non-tangible things have their own vibration, they have a direct effect on our mind and body's frequency; we must be very mindful of our thoughts and feelings because they change the metaphysical make-up and energetic composition of our bodies, which is why thoughts and feelings can create dis-ease in the body. Let's look at emotions and how they affect your vibration.

THAT FEELS SO GOOD

One of the first and most valuable things I learnt from my coach when I embarked on my journey back to my true self was the importance of our emotions. Society today is so quick to shut our emotions down. We are meant to be permanently happy and if we aren't it's deemed 'not good'. We see everyone on social media permanently happy and wondering why we aren't always feeling that. First, let me tell you, it's okay, you don't always have to feel happy, that is an unrealistic constant state of being, and second, don't kid yourself – that person on social media who has posted their best shot is probably having a terrible day but put on a big cheesy smiley because a stroppy face isn't going to cut it. Social media is an illusion and it's time to wise up to it and stop using it as a way of punishing ourselves for what we aren't doing, being and seeing. I will talk more about social media later on in the book. For now, it's back to the matter of emotions and the fact is, we are born with some key basic emotions and each one has a very real function and each one has its own frequency. Feelings are our bodies' GPS system and when a feeling comes up, it's there to tell us something. It is how our body talks to us.

Many of us have lost touch with our feelings and we use a variety of ways to numb them out and push them away so we can pretend to be that permanently 'happy' person society is conditioning us to be.

Imagine for a moment that our feelings are like a telephone and various people keep ringing with a different message and every time they call, you either put the phone on mute, turn the phone off, or direct them to answerphone. They are going to keep calling, aren't they? And if you keep ignoring it, eventually they are going to rock up at your front door, pretty annoyed with a big mouthful to give you. Well, my dear, that's what we are doing each and every day when we ignore our feelings. But how about we listened to our feelings instead of judging them as good, bad or ugly?

I have already discussed shame, now let me tell you a bit about the other emotions and why we have them.

ANGER – ONE LETTER SHORT OF DANGER

Anger is an intense emotion. It involves a strong, uncomfortable and hostile response to a perceived provocation, hurt or threat. It is used as a protective mechanism to cover up fear, hurt or sadness. We use it to feel power-ful when actually we are power-less. Rage, also known as wrath, is slightly different; this is linked to old emotions usually from early childhood when one has felt intense powerlessness which has been suppressed and has come out in later life.

I suffered from anger and rage at times when I first became a mum. It was nothing to do with my son or the situation, it was simply the thing that brought it up and the catalyst for change – thankfully. I felt out of control and powerless, I had no tools to lean on and felt like a lost little girl. Once I understood the source of this, I could dialogue with that part of me that once felt hopeless and helpless. The more I did it, the more balanced and at one I felt. If you are suffering from bouts of anger, tune in to your past and feel about for when you have felt lost, broken, powerless, hopeless or helpless or all of these things. This is where the work needs to be done. At the start of my healing I used an excellent anger meditation to safely release any pent-up anger that was coming up for healing.

Next time you come across a person with intense anger, remember that underneath that anger is hurt and sadness but it has been used to make the person feel powerful. Dig deep and see that person with empathy and compassion. We were all born good people and they don't want to be angry, they are just an incredibly hurt child underneath it all.

Anger is often more hurtful than the injury that caused it and when we use it, in an unhealthy way, we pass on the injury (energy) to another and the cycle continues. Heal the anger, understand its source and you are free from it. Anger need not be something you live with every day. Even frustration such as road rage is unprocessed anger which you are projecting onto another. Just like feeling frustrated and annoyed about your partner never clearing up their mess: the chances are your reaction is disproportionate and you are simply projecting your inner anger onto an external source in a way to disconnect from it. Blame is the same – it's much easier to blame another as opposed to looking inside of yourself. So, ask yourself today, what are you angry about? Really angry about? Dig deep, darling.

FEEL THE FEAR

Fear is an emotional response brought on by a perceived threat. It is what brings on the fight or flight response as well as the 'freeze' reaction. All three are ingrained behaviours that we use to protect ourselves if we deem something or someone to be a threat. Thousands of years ago, we used fear to protect ourselves from wild animals; just like deer who get caught in the head lights we would either freeze and hope the threat went away or we would run away into the woods. Nowadays, we don't have to defend ourselves in the same way we used to, instead we now use fear to protect us from feeling pain, a wound or someone else but our response is the same – we shut down emotionally (freeze), use aggression to defend ourselves (fight) or run away from it (flight), either physically or with the help of alcohol, drugs, shopping and or social media as I mentioned earlier in the book.

What do you fear? Be honest with yourself. What are you afraid of? I spoke about fear earlier in the book, when I showed you that fear really is just an illusion and a set of stories that we have told ourselves. When you understand what you fear and then why it is there, you can let it go. It's about dialoguing with that part of you that in the past has perceived threat and is now doing anything to protect that wound and avoid feeling that feeling again.

Remember we are conditioned to move away from pain and towards pleasure,[3] it is our basic, fundamental programming. Therefore if we perceive a threat, we will do anything to avoid the pain (at all costs) thanks to our subconscious programming. Fear stops us feeling the perceived threat, wound or pain by keeping us away from it. This can manifest in procrastination and avoidance in general, which can be emotional or physical avoidance.

These days so many people live in fear and this is the opposite feeling to love. It is love that we need to return to in every situation, every choice and every view that we have on life. It is here that we have lost our way. Marianne Williamson talks about this and illustrates it so well in her book *Return to Love* where she says, 'Love is what we are born with. Fear is what we learn. The spiritual journey is the unlearning of fear and prejudices and the acceptance of love back in our hearts. Love is the essential reality and our purpose on Earth. To be consciously aware of it, to experience love in ourselves and others, is the meaning of life.'

---

[3] Copyright Marisa Peer

She goes on to give the most beautiful quote, one that at one point really resonated with me, about how exactly she sees fear: 'Our deepest fear is not that we are inadequate. Our deepest fear is that we are powerful beyond measure. It is our light, not our darkness that most frightens us. We ask ourselves, "Who am I to be brilliant, gorgeous, talented, fabulous?" Actually, who are you not to be?' Quite right, who are we not to be? Quite simply playing small does not serve the world. Allowing yourself to be small and shrink just so that others won't feel inadequate around you is not serving you or the world. It's about being a beacon of light and shining by example. Feel the fear and then turn it to love, love of yourself and your capabilities.

Fear has been at my side for most of my life. Every choice that I have made, everything I have done or not done has been from a place of fear. I was even scared of myself and probably my shadow too (certainly my shadow self – the darker sides of ourselves). I remember my coach asking me what I was scared of. 'Say the first thing that comes to your mind, Cat.' 'My power.' Wow, did I really just say that? I didn't even know I felt that! But it was true, I wasn't used to shining or living my truest, fullest and most powerful self. I was used to being broken, needy, weak, and small. It is so true, we are fearful of sharing our true gifts because we may be judged, shamed and made to feel guilty for being our truest, gifted self. Why? Does this feel right to you? Certainly doesn't to me. I truly believe that everyone is here on this planet to share their gift and every single person has a gift, they just forgot how to show it off, or they never got a chance to fulfil their purpose, or when they did, others didn't like it and they learnt that in order to stay safe, they must play small. If this is you, drop this fear today. It is your birthright to fulfil your potential, share your gift with the world and shine bright. You don't need permission to do this and you can start today. This fear isn't protecting you; thank it for doing its job all these years but now it's time to let go of it and to step forward into your very own spotlight. F*ck fear! Let's do this!

There are gifts to fear and these come in the form of protection. It has been there to protect but once we understand that we are no longer that powerless little child that needs protection from the original scenario or feeling, we can let it go.

NO PAIN – NO GAIN

The International Association for the Study of Pain defines *pain* as 'an unpleasant sensory and *emotional* experience associated with actual or potential damage'. This can come in the form of hurt and feelings of sadness and even loneliness. When we feel pain in our bodies, it is like an open wound from the past that is ready and ripe for healing. There have been times in my process where my sadness is like a deep-set pain in my stomach, not like stomach ache as such but you literally feel it as an emotional pain rather than an overtly physical pain, although it is a physical sensation.

I believe that often when someone feels pain in a part of their bodies, they go straight for the medical reason, rather than understanding how a certain unprocessed negative emotion has resided in their body. A study was done mapping our bodies like an atlas and plotting where our basic emotions resided within our bodies using a heat map. For example, anger was located in the chest and head – which is why we say someone is 'hot-headed'! With this in mind, it is widely believed that these unprocessed and suppressed emotions reside within certain organs in our bodies. Again, anger gets stored in the liver and it's no coincidence when someone has liver disease that they have lived a life with repressed, suppressed anger. Remember, dis-ease in the body leads to disease.

The gift of pain is that it alerts you to a physical and emotional issue that has a deeper core feeling underneath it. It creates an awareness and understanding and as we know, knowledge is power. Simply bringing one's awareness to the site of pain will diminish and repair the wound. I like to give the pain a colour and shape and imagine it dissolving while I send it love and healing vibes – believe me, this stuff works. Give it a go.

DON'T TAKE THE GUILT TRIP

As most of us know it, guilt is the fact of having committed a specified or implied offence or crime. It is an emotion that people experience because they're convinced they have caused harm. In cognitive theory, the thoughts cause the emotions. The guilt of emotion follows directly from the thought that you are responsible for someone else's misfortune, whether or not this is the case. It is a man-made emotion and is based on an attachment to another's judgement and an untrue story we tell ourselves and as a consequence make ourselves feel terrible and 'racked with guilt'.

We hold on to guilt from childhood. I had a client once who felt overall not enough and in session she went back to a scene when she was about 7 years old and by mistake killed a hamster. She had done it by accident but was mortified by it and had held this feeling of guilt inside her body for over 40 years. Following the illuminating moment, I got her to write on a piece of paper all the things she had ever felt guilty for. Once she had done that, I got her to rip up the piece of paper and let the feelings of guilt go. She felt liberated by not only sharing what she had felt guilty for but also by actively releasing it.

Guilt is a story we tell ourselves and it gets bigger and bigger the greater the story is that we tell ourselves. It's another of those fabricated things. Most of the time we are telling ourselves a tall story that isn't really the factual one, as we often don't know how we have made another feel or think and guilt is based on the perception of being responsible for someone else's misfortune, even if we aren't.

Of course, guilt is often invoked and used by someone to manipulate and gain control which then plays in to the stories we tell ourselves – this is known as the guilt trip. I like to think of it like someone has tripped us up with their manipulation of a situation. Essentially, it is used to make someone feel guilty, especially in order to induce them to do something that will benefit the other.

The gift of it is, it gives you boundaries and ensures we are operating in our zone of what we deem to be acceptable and honest treatment of others. When we step out of that and believe we have caused hurt or pain, whether it's emotionally or physically, we feel guilt, which serves to remind us to maintain healthy relationships.

<u>HIGH VIBE FEELINGS</u>

Right, time to move on to some lighter feelings now! Remember, if we cut off from our negative emotions and don't allow ourselves to feel anger, pain or sadness, we cut off from our positive ones too – it doesn't differentiate between the good and bad and we end up disconnected and emotionless. When we let go of the above emotions from our mind and body, we make space for lighter, brighter feelings and I am testament to this. We have to feel all the feelings, good and bad. I was riddled with anger, resentment and bitterness. If I stubbed my toe or dropped a plate, the anger that would ooze out of me was tangible. It was easier to project this onto an action or person, but when I learnt where my deep-set emotions had originated and let them go – mostly through crying (the water of the soul) and my trusty anger meditation – I made way for love, joy, peace and happiness.

SPRINKLE JOY AND HAPPINESS EVERYWHERE

Happiness is an emotion in which one experiences feelings ranging from contentment and satisfaction to bliss and intense pleasure. Joy is stronger than that and is a less common feeling than happiness. It is elation, exuberance, blissful contentment and you feel it all over your body and particularly in your heart, rather like it is exploding out of your heart chakra and enveloping you with this blissful blanket of warmth and wonderfulness! That's how I see it, anyway!! How much joy are you experiencing in your life? Are you consumed with anger, guilt and shame that leaves little energetic space in your body for joy? Explore it. When I had let go of the heavier emotions, I was taken aback by how much lighter I felt and looked, literally! I opened my body up to feelings of genuine joy. Now this isn't a sustainable state and nor is happiness because, as I mentioned, the heavier emotions described earlier have a use, we need them to keep us functioning within our boundaries and moral codes. However, we could all do with letting go of those suppressed and deep stuck emotions from the past and bringing forward space for happiness and joy. We deserve this. Happiness and joy aren't allocated to those who are more privileged, more this, more that; they are for everyone but it's down to us to actively seek and achieve them and this comes from deep inner work, not just running away and travelling around the world. That may bring short-term happiness, but it's about honouring our old stories and moving the energy in our bodies which literally makes way for high vibrating feelings.

PASSION IS THE FASHION

'My mission in life is not merely to survive,
but to thrive; and to do so with some passion,
some compassion, some humour,
and some style.'

– Maya Angelou

The key word in this is passion. How many of us are living a life full of things we are passionate about? Or are we just waking up at 7am, going to work, doing a job we hate, getting back on the train to go home, to go to bed to get up at 7am again the next morning, Monday to Friday, for fifty odd weeks a year? This isn't living a life of passion and so many of us are missing the point to life. Passion is key to our existence, it is a high vibrating emotion that makes us feel alive. You know that feeling when you are talking about something you love, something you are passionate about it, it's like a force you can't contain, it's overflowing from you because you are so excited about it. Just like when you take up a hobby, and you are in it and I mean IN IT, you're just loving it because you are passionate about what you are doing.

When I looked up the dictionary meaning of it: it said, 'a strong and barely controllable emotion'. This makes me think of those moments when you are in the throes of passion, when you are wild, uncontained, beholden to this strong and powerful emotion.

> *'Passion is energy.*
> *Feel the power that comes from*
> *focusing on what excites you.'*
>
> - Oprah Winfrey

Yes, Sister! Fuck the low vibe emotions and let's get high vibe and all passionate about life, about waking up each morning, about fulfilling your purpose, about you as a person. Time to unblock your stuck, old, stinky energy and let the joy, happiness and passion run through your veins, like wild horse running through fields. How dreamy and even a little sexy!

The fact is, the more passionate you are about you, your work, your life, or whatever it is you are doing, the more positive energy you are going to feel coursing through your body. Real happiness comes when you do what you are most passionate about. It shapes our existence, fuels the fires of inspiration and opens us up to opportunities and changes around us. It is about having enthusiasm and excitement for life. When we are inspired, we are in-spirit. This is our raw, truest self and purpose. I feel passionate and excited just writing this, my fingers are frantically tap-tapping on the keys because I can feel the energy in my body about this topic and key emotion to fulfilment.

Passion comes when you are being your authentic self and doing what comes naturally to you and in order to feel passion we need to strip away the layers that are stopping us from being true, real, authentic, open, honest. We need to locate our gift and show the world, but we need the confidence to do it. The bottom line is, when what you do is in alignment with who you are, you get energy from doing it and it fills you up no end.

You are my passion. So is this book, so is sharing my message and helping guide other women to their greatest self, their true self, the one they were born as, brimming with confidence, purpose and set for a life of ultimate fulfilment. All of that is in you, you just need to dig deep, peel away some layers, raise your vibrations and you're there. I can feel the energy running through your body as you read this. I know you're ready, you were born ready, darling. I'm so honoured to be by your side as you find your passion, purpose and true self.

Let's focus on all the things that could and will go right as of today. Children are symbols of this raw and real belief in opportunities. They are passionate about the smallest things, they squeal with delight at the slightest thing. We still have that little child in us, let's connect with her and reactivate her passion for life.

> *'Children are happy because they don't*
> *have a file in their minds called*
> *"All the Things That Could Go Wrong".'*

- Marianne Williamson

DO EVERYTHING WITH LOVE

Love...hmmmm... where do I start? Love is... so many things. When I began writing this part of the book, I started with explaining that we have some key, basic emotions and love is one of them. Love is far from basic. Love is complex. Wonderful. All encompassing. It is felt through the whole of the body and it originates from the heart. It is the key to life. When we move away from a place of love, we are out of alignment. We are beings of light and love, not hate and fear (as society is indoctrinating us to believe).

As I see it, love is not a feeling or an emotion, it is an expression of all warm and fuzzy feelings in a single word. In the same way, if you say you love someone, it's not love, it is a mix of emotions like happiness, joy, care, protection and many other emotions and feelings that you describe in a single word called LOVE.

Remember I said at the start of this book, our hearts are the first things created in our bodies; not our brain – our heart. It is the beginning and end of us, it is the place of real truth, real direction. The state of our heart, and our ability or inability to give or receive love, represents the state of our mind and body as a whole. A healthy, open heart that gives and receives love easily and openly is a heart that is untouched and is representative of a healthy and open mind and body. Love is our natural state. We are love and the moment we step away from it, we are moving in the wrong direction. I could go on and on about love but I won't. Just remember, if you are coming from a loving, authentic and honest place with an open heart, you're doing just fine. Love is you. It is the place and emotion you must always go back to. It is our essence. We must vibrate at the frequency of love. High vibe, full of love. That's you. Get back to you, a being of warm and fuzzy, snuggly love that oozes from every pore, and is in every thought and action you take through life. You are love.

YOUR BODY – THE HOUSE OF YOUR EMOTIONS

Let's explore where you feel those feelings in your body but first close your eyes and imagine the last time you fell in love. Maybe you were out at dinner, looking into each other's eyes over a treacle sponge. Where did you feel the love? Perhaps you got butterflies in your stomach or your heart raced with excitement. I have talked about anger being felt in the upper body, chest and head and residing in organs such as the liver.

Fear is another emotion that is felt in the chest, as a tight chest feeling – but it has a different sensation from that of anger. Anger is more explosive, whereas fear feels restrictive and tight. Doctors treat with medicine and often ignore the causes of symptoms but this is a good place to start if you are looking for healing. Illness, however mild or severe, is an indicator of your emotional state, caused by your thoughts and focus. Where you bring focus, you can bring healing. What are you suffering with at the moment? Start to notice where you are suffering in the body and research the link to what emotions get stored where. You'll be amazed. This is the start of understanding the mind-body link.

Once you can identify a feeling in your body, you can understand what your body is telling you and what you need to do in order to honour the feeling. You see, emotions are energy and energy has to go somewhere. Many people numb feelings with alcohol and drugs, but there are other less obvious ways people numb out feelings, such as food, shopping, social media, exercise, even work! Yep, you heard me. Hands up who uses going to work as a way of avoiding feeling a feeling and keeping themselves so busy that they have no time to truly stop and feel? Ever heard of a person who is mourning the loss of a loved one who throws themselves back into work? Well, that person is doing it to divert their mind and avoid the feelings they don't want to feel. Remember, if you keep ignoring that mate (the feeling) on the telephone, they are going to keep ringing or pestering you somehow. The feeling will lodge deeper in your body and eventually disease and disharmony will manifest, your vibration will lower and you won't feel yourself.

So next time when you feel a sensation (which represents a feeling) in your body, in your gut, your chest, your heart, a tension in your head (suppressed anger), notice where it is, bring an awareness to it, honour it, identify it and acknowledge it (by giving it a colour and a shape). This is your body talking to you. Breathe through the sensation, do not numb it – you know the consequences of that. Allow all the stored, old energy (emotion) to arise, notice it, allow it, be open and surrender. It may feel uncomfortable but this is the only way to free yourself of the emotions. Come away from putting stories around the feelings. Humans love a good story, it takes them away from the feeling the discomfort because we tell ourselves a story that readjusts our minds to be able to accept the feeling and situation. By blaming another or projecting our emotion onto another, it stops us having to feel it. Don't play the blame game. Just sit with the feeling, meditate on it, breathe through it. When you master this, you will begin your route to freedom.

'It takes courage to endure the sharp pains of self-discovery rather than choose to take the dull pain of unconsciousness that would last the rest of our lives.'

Have courage, sweet one; the rewards are great, a lifetime of freedom, love and life awaits. I will hold your hand today, tomorrow and always. You've got this, you are courageous.

☆ Here is a valuable list to locate the various emotions in your body:

Anger – All over body, head (hot-headed)

Fear – Tightness in chest, stomach (butterflies)

Pain – Heart and chest (tightening, restricted)

Shame – Face (blushing), neck and upper chest

Guilt – Shoulders, back (carrying a burden, heaviness)

Joy – All over body (sense of lightness)

Passion – Powerful energy throughout, can be sexual

Love – Heart, chest (warm and fuzzy feeling).

When we understand our emotions, we can let them go, release the energy and become more in tune with our gut instinct, our intuition. I once read, 'Gut feelings are your guardian angels sending you messages'. It's so true, as soon as I released the first wave of emotions that I had been suppressing and depressing, I was so much more in tune with my gut. It was like a superpower had been handed to me. Truth is, I always had this superpower, I had just dulled it down. So time now to step up, get your superpower pants on and get all Superwoman on me. Remember, 'Never underestimate the power of a woman's intuition, it's her secret weapon.' Don't you know it! Let's dial that shit back up! We have more of these superpowers, which we will explore in Step 3.

WHAT IS YOURS IS NOT MINE

The world of energy is a fascinating thing and one that I have spent hours and hours exploring and understanding. Just because we can't see it, doesn't mean it doesn't exist. We've all had those moments when you're sitting calmly and happily in a room with others, then another person walks in and within seconds, without even speaking, they have changed the whole feel of the room. Their energy has completely altered the resting state of the room. You know, like when your boss enters the room and you can just 'sense' there is something up, they are stressed, frantic, and their nervous system is hyper-aroused and they haven't even said anything! That's energy speaking. Empaths are those who have an amazing ability to read and perceive other people's energy and mental state because they are hypersensitive to other people's emotions. This can be a great gift (another superpower of sorts) but it can also be a curse because when you can read another person's energy at the drop of a hat, it can get messy – it can prove tricky to differentiate what is your energy and what you are feeling from another.

When babies are young, including in the womb, they don't understand language. Their modes of communication and reading what is taking place in a room is by means of energy. That's why babies can be sensitive to changes in a room and the people in it – we've all witnessed that embarrassing moment when they are handed to a relative and have an impromptu meltdown. Yep, that's energy again. They can sense and feel far more than we (non-empaths) feel. This continues through childhood until you slowly shut this ability down or disassociate from this superpower, though the truth is that we still all have this skill but it needs fine tuning.

With this in mind, I want to show you how much we have absorbed from our parents as we grew up, in a positive and negative sense. We begin to absorb and become aware of energy around us from our very early days on Earth and even the womb, when we can sense sensation and feelings from our mother. Our subconscious stores everything and remembers all these feelings and times when you were around your mother and she felt overwhelmed, depressed, happy, sad, mad and glad. I often do a deep visualisation with my clients when I take them back to the hospital room when they were born and get them to explore what the scene was: What was mum feeling and thinking? Where were they as a newborn baby? What were they thinking and feeling? How was mum's energy making them feel? Loved or not? Overwhelmed, unwanted or wanted? Almost 100% of my clients who I have done this with will have come to me with feelings of overwhelm, stress, and feelings of loneliness; and when I take them back to the hospital room, their present feelings match those experienced by their mum in the hospital room and then become their own feelings.

Of course, it's not just our mums that we absorb things from; fathers and siblings play their part too. What was dad like when you grew up? Was he stressed, angry, absent emotionally? What did you absorb from him? Did he have financial worries and problems at work? What was he bringing home that you could feel, even if he didn't tell you he felt this way? What about your parents' relationship, whether or not they were together. What was going on behind closed doors that they weren't telling you but you could feel all of it and more? Children are highly sensitive and empathic beings – do not underestimate what you felt and absorbed as a child in your household. If you are a parent now, start to notice what you are feeling and how amazingly your child will play out what you are feeling inside. Maybe you're not angry on the outside but inside you feel frustrated and there is something on your mind and then before you know it, your kids are fighting and playing out the feelings that are going on inside you. I explained this to my husband after my coach drew my attention to it. At first he wasn't that convinced but the more he watched, the more he was astounded by this interaction between us. The dance of energy is amazing. Sometimes it takes my children to show me what I really feel inside because I didn't really know myself. Children are great gifts and fantastic teachers if we open up our awareness and begin to notice how our energy is affecting them. They feel what we feel so if I'm happy and clear, so are they. This is why it is so important to do the work on ourselves. Happy parents equals happy kids.

Remember you were a child once and you felt and witnessed all the energy around your family house in your early years, more than you know. Explore this. What was taking place behind those four walls? What did you absorb and feel? What's yours and what isn't? That's the key question here. What was mum's overwhelm and what is rightly yours? What shame and guilt is genuinely yours? I suspect not much. What feelings do you experience mostly as an adult? Ask yourself, what am I feeling? Who does this belong to? Is it mine or another's? Is this yours or is this learnt behaviour and absorbed feelings that you are ready to free yourself from? Darling, you no longer need this burden, you have carried it for way too long. It's time to give back what was never yours. Shame, guilt, anger, sadness, loneliness – let it go, time to release it. Often, when clients come to me with weight issues, it's exactly this, they have been carrying around the burden of emotions that were never theirs in the first place. When I help them see this, it frees them finally and the weight starts to shift like they have let go of their excess baggage.

HAPPY FAMILIES

We love to create a fairy tale in our head about our childhood (I did!) which is far from the reality it was. Now this isn't to say that it was all terrible and you lived like Cinderella, cleaning and scrubbing floors, before she found her shoe! It takes courage to acknowledge and admit that things weren't how you expected them to be – full of love. Maybe your needs were met, maybe they weren't. Maybe dad was around physically but was emotionally absent. Perhaps mum was more absorbed with her career or other siblings to give you the time that you needed. Whatever it is, it's okay. You don't need to dress it up with flowers and fairy lights to make it seem more acceptable. I often have this with clients who come to me feeling a certain way, let's say stressed and like a failing mother or failing at work or in a turbulent relationship. I then take them on a journey back to their early memories and show them why their past has created their present feelings and circumstances. It is always eventually met with relief, even if at first there is resistance or blind denial, and it can take a little time to adjust to the reality rather than the fairy tale.

I have had clients who also shut down and immediately go into feelings of guilt for talking about their parents and seeing things from another perspective. Is this you? Do you think you would find it hard to acknowledge the truth behind your current state of mind? What's the worst that can happen? I always remind my clients that this isn't a witch hunt for what your parents did or didn't do. It's just an exploration into the past to get evidence for why you are feeling like you do now. It's not a judgement of whether they were good, bad, right or wrong. Just a factual and honest understanding of the truth and why that has led to where you are now. The truth is, this life is about you and getting the most from it and that requires you to put your needs first and get you back on track. Yes, that might mean looking at some stuff that may feel a little uncomfortable because you are used to your warm and fuzzy Disney story, or you're used to protecting and hero-ing your parents or siblings. Once you take a look back and get your understanding, you can let it go and move on – you don't need to dwell on it. But in order to heal you must first understand and feel. So for the good of you, open your heart and mind, allow yourself to go back, heal whatever needs to come up and make way for your bright and happy future.

I was very attached to my fairy tale and although I was open to knowing what I felt and why, it took a little time to process and accept that real story. As you read this book, there will be things that prompt your subconscious to bring forward memories and moments and there will also be times when your belief systems are challenging. Beliefs are there to be changed and when you become open to learning with an air of curiosity, it will be on a fast track to healing and remedying your current status quo. Sometimes it might feel like you have had the rug pulled from under your feet and the foundations shaken. It may seem after all these years that the story you have been telling yourself (to make reality feel more bearable) is more like a nightmare. It may feel less rose tinted and more mud splattered. But trust that the time has come to face and heal this, the real story, and take off the rose-tinted glasses.

You picked up this book because part of you needs to heal, you have forgotten your magnificence and you want to change your outlook and create a life you love because currently something isn't working for you. Well, my dear, if you want to change and create, you have to discover first (Step 1). So on with the courageous pants, pop your super-sharp goal-focusing glasses on and buckle up because you have to do 'the work' to get results. Resistance will simply keep you stuck. Denial will stop you achieving your potential. Avoidance will be your loss. Face the past, heal the present and make way for a bright and sunny future, full of passion, energy and smashing the glass ceiling. The world is your oyster, once you face the doo-doo that is keeping you stuck. Go back to your intention and remember why you are doing it, why you are choosing to build a better, more stable foundation that is made up of self-love, the honouring of your emotions, self-care, self-compassion and of course self-acceptance. This is what you live for, not staying put.

Right, now we have got that out the way and you're fully on board and now see the worth and goal of your journey. Let's get serious and really start exploring our early programming. I remember talking to my dear friend Lucy, a fabulous psychologist and wise woman, about how I view healing.

She agreed and used the analogy of our subconscious mind being like a computer and how with a computer we must upgrade the software – you know how Apple loves to send a 'software update' to your iPhone. Well, so it is with our mind. It needs upgrading: our beliefs and our early programming need a big reboot. Now we can wait until a breakdown, death, birth, implosion or divorce (mine was a birth, two actually!) or we can acknowledge that every single one of us has picked up unwanted behaviours, thoughts, belief systems, habits and more from our early years. You are running on an old operating system and it's time to stop postponing the upgrade, click the button, make space for the new operating system and open yourself up to a new way of working.

We have been socially conditioned by the media, school, family, parents, teachers, siblings, friends of family, grandparents and so on and have been told 'you are this, you are that, you're meant to be this, this behaviour is acceptable, this career is right, this is wrong, money is evil, abundance is unattainable, life is short, we are finite, blonde is best, thin is sexy, pert breasts are lush!' You get me. Well, it's time now to untether those beliefs that weren't yours in the first place, we were just told how to think and what to think.

IT STARTS IN THE FAMILY

We are born into a dynamic that we have no choice over. It just is. Life begins in your early years set-up, whether that is with a family, early caregivers, or a single parent – it all starts here. Where do you see your place in the family set-up? (I'm calling it family in a loose sense – it can be a care home, foster family, whatever it looks like). What was your role? What early beliefs did you form? I shared some of mine in the introduction (my story) – they were my story but not anymore. I felt insignificant in my family set-up. I felt small, in the physical sense of being the youngest and the only girl but also in the sense that it was easier to be out of sight, playing by the rules, quiet and perfect. If I stuck to the rules then Mummy and Daddy would love me and I would get connection that way. Well, this wasn't true but it was the role I decided to play in order to give myself the best opportunity to be accepted in the family dynamic and ultimately safe. What role have you assumed? What traits does this role come with?

I remember Marisa Peer, my wonderful hypnotherapist teacher, educating me about the roles in a family.[4] She states, there are four clear roles with a family set-up.

The nurse - who likes to care for people and gets their worth from this; caring for others creates connection and self-worth.

The rebel - who gets connection by playing up, negative attention is better than no attention; it also singles them out and makes them different.

---

[4] Copyright Marisa Peer

The achiever - the kid that does brilliantly at everything; they get their worth from being great and from attention for their accomplishments.

The sick one - who gets connection, touch and attention from being unwell.

Which one are you? Or are you the fifth child for whom there is no role? Did you feel lost, like there was no role for you? Which role are your siblings or parents playing?

I was the carer. I took on everyone else's pain, not because they made me but because I found that the best place to be – when Mum was feeling down, I did whatever I could to make her feel better. Similarly, if my brother was sad as a kid, I would do the same and want to care for his needs. It's no surprise that I now do what I do and I continue to help others. But the difference is, I do it in a healthy dynamic and I don't seek to get my worth from it. I am worthy without it. I am worthy just as I am, in that role or not.

It's pretty eye-opening and it is so true: start to notice which role you have been playing all this time, because you no longer need to play it. Others get so used to us playing this, it suits them, it works for them and ultimately benefits their needs but absolutely not yours. Where are you playing that role and putting others' needs before yours? Where are you playing that role and resenting it? Where are you playing that role and feeling suffocated by it?

Not only was I playing the role of a carer but, as I mentioned before, I was playing small. On top of this, as I grew I learnt that if I played the damsel in distress, I would get attention. Usually from a hero in the form of Dad in a financial but non-emotional sense, Mum in an emotional sense and, later on, from my husband emotionally. Being broken or a damsel in distress worked for me – I got connection, attention and I got rescued. Why would I want to be anything else? Well in the end, broken was so broken, no one could save me except myself. And that is what my journey has been all about – learning to shine and rescue myself with love, compassion and acceptance. Here I stand as my own heroine, shining like a star, speaking my truth (in the form of this book and workshops) and being me, masks off, true self, here I am.

Do you *really* want to save yourself? Or is it serving you to stay stuck, small, or a victim?

Listen here, Sister, and listen good! You have a special gift: you are gorgeous, unique, you have a passion-filled purpose all inside of you that the world wants and needs to see. Wake up! Stop staying stuck, time is up! We have a job to do on this Earth. Patriarchy has dominated for far too long. The world needs compassion, love and understanding and these are the feminine traits. The world needs you to stop playing to the patriarchy roles or damsels in distress, or hiding your light because you might fail, get shamed, lose your partner. How about you trusted and in doing so, upgraded your life, changed your future, found your purpose and lived a fulfilled life?

I cannot express to you enough the benefits of detoxing your emotions. Rather like every spring we need to clear out the cobwebs, dust off the pictures, clean the silver – the same applies to our minds. We have got to go back and dig out the old, dusty, outdated rubbish and add some new bits of sparkle and joy so that we can feel clear, clean, refreshed and ready to take on more challenges. It's rather like shifting energy – out with the old, in with the new. I have shown you the benefits of detoxing your emotions, I am a testament to it and I have changed and upgraded my life immeasurably, and you can too. You have well and truly committed to the upgrade and the benefits and evidence will unfold right before your eyes. It really is that simple. Push through the muddy stuff and on the other side is glitter and sparkles.

MANAGING YOUR INNER FLATMATE

One of the most crippling things I was struggling with prior to my journey was the critical voice inside my head. I remember a few months before I began work with my coach, I turned to a friend and said, 'I just hate myself so much.' I was consumed by this self-loathing and it followed me around everywhere. I noticed it mostly when it came to food and the way that I spoke to my body. Although I never had a problem with my weight, I noticed that I would abuse my body by over-eating, under-eating, eating food with little or no nutritional value. It wasn't necessarily the amount that I was over- or under-eating but more the words that went with the act. The truth was, it wasn't really about my body or the food, this was just my vehicle for self-loathing. What vehicle are you using to project your stuff onto – exercise, work, food, alcohol? And what is the script that goes with it? Who or what is on the receiving end of your feelings of inadequacy or anger? Be honest.

To project is to blame and at the time it feels much easier to blame another person or thing for the reason why you feel like you do. But I ask you to stop for a moment and truly ask yourself: is this about something now or are you really projecting an old emotion onto a current situation? More often than not, it will be an old, recycled emotion that has come up for healing. Only about 5% of it will be about the current situation – your boss being an arsehole or your partner being non-communicative and distant. It took me a while to really be honest with what I was projecting and what was really happening now. In the end, I learnt that pretty much Every. Single. God-damn time, it was an old emotion that my subconscious had held on to and had loosely matched the current situation to the old one. In order to move past this, you must go back to the original memory that has been triggered. Does your arsehole of a boss remind you of a strict parent or caregiver? Does your emotionally absent partner remind you of your emotionally absent sibling, parent or such like from way back when? Stop and take notice. Bring an awareness to that pattern of behaviour.

My inner chat was deafening and almost debilitating at times. How could I stop this? The first step was the discovery part – once I knew why I was frustrated with myself, I knew it was an old thought and feeling and wasn't what I truly felt at the present time. The more I learnt about myself the more I let go of the negative self-talk. By bringing an awareness to the chatter meant I was halfway to healing it. The more I understood it, the more I could work with it.

It's quite common for authors and creatives alike to experience this nagging self-talk: Who am I to share my message, write a book, paint this canvas, stand on stage? What's your negative self-talk and what is stopping you from doing? When clients come to me with negative internal chatter, I explore with them who this voice belongs to, because, hear this, it's not yours! Yep, you heard me! That little voice that resides inside your head is like an annoying negative flatmate. They are always there, in your space, with negative chatter in your ear at the end of a long day. The voice is weighing you down, getting on your nerves, keeping you small, stopping you from fulfilling your dreams and achieving your goals. But whose voice is it really?

Let's explore, is it masculine or feminine? What are they saying? At what moments are they loudest? Is it mum or dad's voice, or maybe it's a teacher, grandparent, nanny, sibling or key caregiver from your early days? The most important thing you need to know is that voice is NOT yours! Remember, you came into this world full of confidence and it was only life's experiences that you have attached to and they have become you. You are a being of light and love, of pure consciousness. You are not your story, you are not your beliefs, thoughts or feelings. You are pure magic with a gift to share with this world. You are limitless and abundant with so much to give.

Whenever you hear that negative self-talk, acknowledge it and simply thank it. A little tool to use when that negative chatter comes in or you hear yourself berating yourself for making a mistake, say 'thank you for sharing' or even 'nullify' as soon as you notice yourself uttering the words of discontent. This immediately cuts the connection between the words and yourself. Another good one is if you wear an elastic band on wrist and ping it every time you say something negative about yourself. The ping will sting a bit but it will quickly cut the negative pattern of thought.

Don't give away your power to it. They are not your thoughts, you have picked these up from someone who felt, and no doubt still feels, inadequate, and by keeping you small and not enough, it stops them from feeling even more not enough! Whoever that person's voice is that you have attributed it to, notice how it is them who felt not enough and how it would be if you were brimming with enoughness? It would feel rather uncomfortable for them but that's their story. You are choosing to let go of this part of you. It was never yours.

You are now choosing to stand in your power, not be pulled in to their world.

This is why as a parent, or anyone interacting with children, it is so important to be a positive role model and be mindful of the words, labels and beliefs that you spill onto a child. Children are like sponges and they pick it all up and it becomes them and then they spend their adulthood living or undoing the early beliefs that were forced upon them.

As soon as I understood my early programming I could begin to make friends with that sad and hurt part of me. I dialogue a lot with my inner child which also is a great tool to re-pair those parts of me and my mind that have been subjected to hurtful words. The stories and words that you have been telling yourself are the old script. Rip it up, burn it, put it in the rubbish, because, girlfriend, that shit is not yours! Onwards and upwards, goodbye old story, hello new one!

ROLE MODELS

You have now acknowledged your inner critic and are beginning to find ways to manage it. It's now time to pick some positive role models to inspire you and aspire to. As kids, we are incredibly malleable and we mould ourselves to the key people in our lives in order to gain connection and acceptance, most notably from our parents. Who were your role models as a kid? Did you look up to someone and, if so, what were their character traits and beliefs? When we analyse the key people in our life and how they fit with the intention that you came with at the start of the book, you may find some discrepancies. What do I mean by that? Let me explain: if you have set your intention to having a creative business that is successful, financially abundant and enjoyable to work in, but one or both of your key caregivers worked tirelessly, for little money or joy, moaned a lot about how hard work is and you witnessed how tiring it was and there was little reward, and they didn't spend much time with the family and were generally miserable – the chances are that you have picked up certain beliefs about work, such as that work is hard, you earn little money from it no matter how hard you work, it's not fun, and the list goes on. This has become your subconscious belief system and although you might not consciously feel it, underneath it all, those are the intrinsic belief systems running your show.

Our role models don't necessarily have to be openly negative ones but by becoming and being like them, we passively grow into them without even knowing it. Of course, there are positive role models who will have had profound effects on you and your life and you are gifted to have those people make that impression in your life. For those who weren't lucky enough to have positive role models as a frame of reference, worry not, because you can create your very own positive role models now. The power of a muse is big. Pick someone who is currently living a life that you would like: how does it look and feel? It can be a famous person, for example, who is living a life that you aspire to have; embody their energy and think about how they might react or be in a certain situation. I find Instagram a great place for this; if used in the best way, social media can create an aspirational place to manifest a life you want by showing you visuals of the life you want to create. It's like an ever-evolving, interactive vision board at the tips of your fingers. Note: don't be sucked into the look of a life or lifestyle. Look deeper into their soul and don't be fooled by that false sense of a perfect life just by scrolling through someone's feed. Pick a positive muse and role model – there are plenty of women nowadays owning their power, showing their magic, sharing their gift whether that's in the form of a politician who's making a difference, a mumpreneur, a spiritual teacher, author, or coach. There are so many women now who are standing up, speaking their truth, playing big and sharing their story while they do it, just like me! Better still, be your own role model and write down who you are and be that. Show that little girl inside you how to do it, parent her as you wish you had been parented. It's never too late, start today and rebuild that part of you so that you can take over the world and shine your light.

OWN YOUR SHADOW SIDE

So often in society these days, women are shamed for being emotional, loud, vocal, reactive, or explosive, because good girls don't make a fuss. Well, I have something to say: f*ck that sh*t!

I played perfect for years, 35 years to be precise, and now I choose another story.

Perfectionism is the highest form of abuse because there is no perfect so you will fail every time. If you are suffering or have suffered from this, you know that there is never a point at which you are satisfied. With perfectionism, you never get it perfect or right so you always live like whatever it is you are trying to achieve is not good enough and this 'not good enough' becomes a fundamental belief: 'I am not good enough'. I am a recovered perfectionist. My belief was if I was a good little girl, Mummy and Daddy would love me, spend time with me, give me connection and make me feel enough. As an adult, this drive for perfectionism became all-consuming and then out of control by the time my children arrived on the planet. I was the mum who made the christening cake, the party food, decorated the house, and made home-made, gluten-free, organic cupcakes. The chores and lists I would put together in order to make me feel enough were endless.

This drive for perfectionism also extended to the way I handled my feelings and truth. Perfect girls don't get angry. Perfect girls don't lose their rag. Perfect girls sit quietly and look pretty.

No thanks. Not anymore. Yes, I get angry; yes, I sometimes react or explode with emotion; yeah, OK, my healing can get messy and so can my hair. It's okay to be wild and it's time we honour our shadow side and honour our true selves instead of shaming it. Of course, the aim is enlightenment, when we are observers of emotions, allow our feelings to rise and flow. But in the meantime, stop shutting down the emotional part of you and allow her to show herself in a safe and healthy way. Of course, don't splurge your sh*t over your peers at work or your children, but do not let another person, man, mouse or elephant, tell you to hide your shadow self. Your anger is there for a reason, your feelings are there to be felt. Even jealousy, when it arises is there to tell you something, to show you where work needs to be done. So next time there is a part of you that you feel needs to be shut down and hidden, allow that part of you to be revealed and welcome her forward: this is your shadow side and she is there to tell you something. Listen closely. Honour your shadow side. As Rumi once said, the wound is the place where the light enters. Darkness is your guide, it is your teacher. Don't shut it down.

As I sign off this chapter, I will leave you with this beautiful quote:

'It's rather easy to shine in the light but to glow in the dark, that's mastery.'

– Rick Beneteau.

What have I discovered?

What do I want to change?

What do I want to create?

☆

'Unleash your
inner sparkle.'

Tools for Shedding your Old Skin

chapter three

Darling,

Stop apologising for who you are, for what you stand for and for what you believe in. You have a voice, you have a mission. Don't deny yourself that freedom. Enough of playing small. Rise up, girl. I'm right there with you.

Shine on, Sister!

Always,

Your Self-Esteem

'Once upon time there lived an empowered woman who ignited her spark and wouldn't sit down; she had a job to do and a gift to share!'

An anonymous quote reinterpreted by Me

A lot has been unveiled, you've learnt so much about yourself already. You have lined up your (former) self-limiting beliefs, you can now see yourself in your family dynamic, you're aware of whose energy you have absorbed, who your role models were and what emotions are over-riding and overwhelming you. Now what?

This is where the work begins. It's not enough to know and understand what our stuff is, we have to do the work in order to move through it and let it go. In order to heal, you have to feel. Feel the pain of the past hurts and wrongs. When we feel an emotion as a child, we have often been forced to suppress it and hide what we truly feel so when we are an adult locating what it is that is causing depression or anxiety (however that looks) you have to go back to the feeling. Men are preconditioned to think much more with their left brain, the more logical part of them. Women are much more in their right brain, where our creativity and emotional self resides, therefore it isn't enough to logically understand the past, we have to get into the body, the feeling, the senses, so that we can let go of the memory and feeling associated with it so that eventually when one goes back to that memory there is no emotional charge or energy attributed to it.

As you now know, the subconscious is the computer system that is running your life and, at times, blocking you from moving forward. Even though consciously you want that job, to marry, to be happy, if it doesn't fit with your subconscious programming, your subconscious will block it. So that's why we have to work on releasing and rewiring it.

You have connected with your inner child and now have an understanding of what she is thinking and feeling but we are now going to go deeper and I'm going to show you how powerful this tool is to repair and heal your emotional self.

HEY, BABY CAKES!

Inner child work is one of the oldest and most powerful tools in psychology. Before I embarked on my emotional detox, I had never heard of this and, boy, did I need it! I have already touched on this in Chapter 1 but I want to delve even deeper. What exactly is inner child work? Fear not, it sounds weirder than it is; essentially, it is making the connection to our inner, emotional self. As children, we form beliefs based on many scenarios in our childhood, and as they take place we log the memory and if another scenario takes places similar to that one you logged then they get bundled together until your brain sees a pattern and creates a habit of thought.

This initial scenario might have been a time when a parent dismissed you when you were young, let's say five years old, which led to you feeling unwanted, inadequate and not loved. When this happened again, it triggered the same feeling in you and cemented the initial thought you had told yourself, then it happened for the fifth, sixth, seventh time and before you knew it, your five-year-old self had created a belief – 'I am not wanted, not enough and not lovable.' Fast forward 20 years and a similar scenario takes place where someone acted in a way that made you feel 'not wanted'. This then triggers your adult self and subconscious mind to return to that initial feeling you felt as a five-year-old. Even though you're not necessarily going back to the memory, your cellular memory and body remember the physiological feeling linked to that belief. This five-year-old is your inner child, the child who still holds that memory and belief even when you are an adult.

In order to let go of self-limiting beliefs, one must go back and connect with the inner child or inner children and show them that these present scenes are not linked to the past and that they can let go of those memories and feelings, while repairing and meeting their needs with a huge doses of TLC, kind words and a whole load of love so that eventually the inner child forms new beliefs and, in turn, so does your adult self! Simple!

We were all children once and, believe it or not, we still have that child dwelling within us. However, most adults are quite unaware of this. And this lack of acknowledgement of our inner child is precisely where so many behavioural, emotional and relationship difficulties come from. If only the adults took a long look at themselves and remedied the past, things would look very different. The fact is, the majority of so-called adults are not truly adults at all. It's rather like Tom Hanks' film *Big*, where the little boy wishes to be big and wakes up the next morning to find himself in the body of an adult. So many of society's adults are walking around as little kids in a grown-up's outfit. But this isn't true adulthood. True adulthood is about accepting and taking responsibility for loving and parenting our own inner child. Sadly, for most adults, this never happens. Instead their inner child has been denied, neglected, disempowered, not heard, abandoned and rejected. We are told by society to 'grow up' and put childish things aside. To become adults, we've been taught to hide or dull our innocence, wonder, awe, joy, sensitivity, playfulness and even cheekiness – some adults have even gone as far as killing this part of them (eek, I know, sounds awful but it's true – you should hear about some of my inner children and how I have found them when I first connected with them!). The inner child has all these wonderful traits, but also holds all our build-up of childhood hurt, trauma, pain, fear and anger. Adults are convinced they have successfully outgrown and left this child and its emotional baggage behind, but I'm sorry to tell you, most haven't. When we connect with our inner child we rewrite our past and heal our future. We stop taking the hurt and passing it on to our children. I do this every day, it's part of my self-care.

THE PLAYGROUND AWAITS

Inner child work is a powerful tool in psychology and one I use a lot in my work to help people heal their wounds. The inner child is very real – I don't mean in a physical or literal sense but figuratively, as a figment of your imagination if you like; it is metaphorically real. As Dr Stephen Diamond, a leading psychologist states, 'it is a psychological reality'. Most mental disorders and destructive behaviour patterns are, as Freud first showed us, more or less related to this unconscious part of ourselves and it's this lack of consciousness that is playing havoc with your life and many others out there! Our subconscious mind stores every event, feeling and emotion, and so although we may have been bitten by a spider at the age of five, our adult self will remember this event like it was yesterday. All the same fears, emotions and feelings are activated as if we were five years old all over again. We take that five-year-old's feelings all the way through life until we heal the pain, fear or sadness that they felt.

A majority of so-called adults are not truly adults at all – what a frightening thought! Yes, we all get older in years (hopefully), that's the easy bit; but psychologically speaking, this is not adulthood – we have to take responsibility for loving and parenting our own inner child in order to be a conscious and fully functioning adult. What we are calling 'grown-ups' are people who are unconsciously being influenced by the emotions of our inner child. For so many, it is not an adult running their life, but an emotionally wounded inner child inhabiting a grown-up's body. A five-year-old running around in a 35-year-old body – what a thought! And that's exactly what I was. I had a little hurt girl inside me plus an angry teenager who needed some love, compassion and understanding. They needed to be heard and seen. And until I recognised and acknowledged this part of me, those little versions of me where running the show. When we repair and remedy the inner child and meet her needs, we become a 'functional adult', one who is functioning and behaving how an adult is expected to, making decisions and choices from a calm and balanced view point, responding, not reacting – as opposed to a hot-headed hurt child. How about you? Is there a hurt, angry, fearful little girl calling the shots and attempting to make big adult decisions? How are you handling life when you are sending your little girl (inner child) out into the big wide world to do work? Are you really just an eight-year-old trying to have a grown-up relationship or even marriage? Isn't that a lot to expect from her?

It's no wonder that divorce rates are so high when so many in society are coming from a place of childlike views and feelings. One wonders why these relationships fall apart. Why we feel so anxious. Afraid. Insecure. Inferior. Small. Lost. Lonely. But think about it: how else would any child feel having to fend for themselves in an apparently adult world? Without proper parental supervision, protection, structure, nurture or support?

THE INGREDIENTS FOR SHINING

In order to heal your wounds of the past, you first need to become conscious of your own inner child. Remaining unconscious is what gives power to the dissociated inner child and allows her to take possession of your personality and overpower your will as an adult.

Next, you must learn to take your inner child seriously and to consciously communicate with that little girl within you. You must learn to listen to how she feels and respond to what she needs from you now. The primal needs of your inner child – love, acceptance, protection, nurturing and understanding – are the same today as when you were a child. As so-called adults, the problem is that we look outside of us to our partners, friends, even work colleagues to fulfil our inner child's needs; but it has to come from you, no one else.

While I was writing this book, I had a string of clients come to me feeling overwhelmed and inadequate and when I asked them how they felt, the first thing they would do would be to blame their partners for how they feel – 'My husband does this or he doesn't do that...' This is our first mistake – no one can make us feel a certain way and it is not their job to make you feel whole. This is solely your job to repair that inner wound so that you can have a healthy and adult relationship. If we don't do this, then the relationship is doomed to fail, as the statistics show. What we didn't sufficiently receive in the past from our parents must be confronted in the present, painful though it may be. The past traumas, sadness, disappointments and depression cannot be changed and must be accepted. Becoming an adult means swallowing this 'bitter pill' that, unfortunately for most of us, certain infantile needs were, maliciously or not, unmet by our imperfect parents or caregivers. And they never will be, no matter how good or smart or attractive or spiritual or loving we become. Those days are over. What was done cannot be undone. We should not as adults now expect others to meet all of these unfulfilled childhood needs. They cannot. Authentic adulthood requires both accepting the painful past and the primary responsibility for taking care of that inner child's needs, for being a 'good enough' parent to her now and in the future.

This may all sound ridiculous but trust me, this is going to be a massive game changer for you. It has been my greatest tool in healing myself and continues to be the best way that I remedy any fears or wobbles that I may have. By initiating and maintaining an ongoing dialogue between the two, a beautiful connection and reconciliation between you and your inner child can be reached. A new and healthy relationship can be created in which the sometimes conflicting needs of both the adult and inner child can be fulfilled and satisfied. I have been known to devise board meetings in my head with my adult self and my inner children so that we can move forward together and find ways to do this so all parties are happy!

When you do this, your life will change. You are rewriting the past, healing old wounds and making way for a magnificent future! It is an amazing relationship, although hard at times, which creates a functional adult who understands and accesses that special part of them making way for a happy and understanding adult life. Dig deep and find that little one, listen to that inner child, she is waiting for you.

What is the age of your inner child that is running the show that is called 'your life'? Ask yourself, 'How old do I feel emotionally?' What is she feeling and what does she need? Time to step up and tune in to that little girl within so that you can remind her just how enough she is, how perfect and whole she is and that she is loved unconditionally.

I went back over my client notes from when I set up my practice and, to my astonishment, 95% of my clients suffered from feelings of 'not enough'. Although this manifested in many different ways in their life such as a difficult marriage, poor relationship with food, overwhelm, stress and anxiety, the core beliefs underneath these different manifestations were the same – a belief that they aren't enough. So, if the very least that you do is to remind yourself (and while you do that, your inner child will benefit) that you are so unbelievably enough and always have been and always will be and that no parent or teacher, sibling or peer can make you feel otherwise, then that is enough and will go some way in repairing this little girl's view of herself. I urge you, though, to dig deep and connect on a deeper level if not for you but your children because the chances are that your children are matching the core beliefs that you have deep down inside.

So, you have got the concept of what the inner child is and how it works. But how do you integrate it in to your daily life? Ah, that's the easy bit! When I first set out healing and connecting with my inner child, I did it alongside my coach where she gently guided me to meet my inner child while my eyes were closed. But you can do this yourself, by simply tuning into how old you feel when you are overwhelmed, angry or sad – whatever emotion is present – and thinking back to a time in your childhood when you felt those feelings. This is your first step. Notice what she is doing and wearing but most importantly what is she feeling and why she feels like she does. Feeling not heard is a big trigger for many and this goes back to our time as children when we were shut down and our voice was suppressed. So when you connect with your inner child it's really important to let her talk to you and express what she is feeling. In response, listen. Allow whatever is meant to come up, listen closely, earn her trust, tell her you are sorry that she has felt that way for all these years and that you are there for her now. This is about turning up and re-parenting her and meeting her needs that weren't met as a child so that you can begin to live as a functional adult rather than an adult who is living from child's perspective. You are showing up for her now, after all these years, to support and love unconditionally. You are there to keep her safe and support her through her growth. Remember: watch out for that critical voice popping in your head telling you this is load of cow testicles. If it comes up, be sure to reply 'Thanks for sharing' or just ping your elastic band.

This is a life-long connection and as you grow as an adult, setting greater goals, following bigger dreams, other moments will come up where that little girl in you will need reassurance and love, support and connection. This is your greatest tool and go to – as you heal her, you heal you. This is about re-pairing your connection so you become whole, one, united, and, in doing so, shine your light.

In my early days of connecting with my inner child I would do long visualisations where I would talk to her while creating a safe space in my mind. I would also use a guided meditation. There are some great ones out there including in the free resources that come with this very book! Nowadays, I can be anywhere at all – in the car, sitting on the toilet, waiting for my kids to put their shoes on, and I can connect with my inner child at any time in my mind. It's not always the age of the one that you first met, I have many ages that I connect with – we are quite a tribe now! As you grow and continue on your journey of self-discovery, different parts of you will come forward from different times in your childhood. Locate the age you feel and go from there – she is waiting for you and together you heal and repair.

Once a dialogue is formed and you have formed a relationship with her based on trust, understanding and a sense of openness, you can take this further and start to reminisce about what she loves doing. This little girl in you is infinitely creative and has ideas that will blow your mind. If you are a mum, auntie, friend or godmother to young children, you have seen how imaginative and gifted they are – well, hear me now, you are too. You still have those qualities within you – you just need to reactivate them. This is the fun part!

Let her take you down memory lane and show you the things she loves to do. Perhaps it's drawing, painting, roller-skating – whatever it might be. And then I challenge you to take up that hobby again. Creativity mixed with fun brings joy to us and keeps us young. When we reactivate this part of us, we awaken a part of us that has been dormant and shut down for whatever reason – maybe it was a negative teacher or parent. Take that inner child by the hand and buy yourself a colouring book or a pair of roller-skates and see what happens when you do this. Or perhaps, you already do something that sets your soul alight but you need to commit to it regularly. Are you at a point in your life where you hate your job, you're fed up with the graft and monotony of the 9–5? If this is you, wakey wakey sunshine! I prescribe a deep connection with your inner child so that you can reactivate that fun, joyous, carefree part of you that is in there somewhere – you just have to dig deep because time is up. You deserve to feel those feelings of love and joy, to experience fun like you did as a child. Remember back then when the simple things brought you joy? Being by the sea, running through the forest, climbing trees, splashing in puddles, being in nature – all these things heal and reactivate that simple child within.

TRAUMA - THE TIME FOR GROWTH

As you are reading this, I can hear you saying, 'Well, Cat, that's all very well but my stuff is much deeper than all this and a few visualisations aren't going to crack this'. Of course, I would never want to cover up a wound and ignore any deep stuff that's going on for you and it's really important to have the right help and only you can know what you need and where you start, but it's starting that is important. Often I guide a client to go to see a counsellor or psychotherapist first to get a logical grip on what is coming up for them so that essentially the top layer of the scum is scraped off, so the real work begins. But remember also, you don't have to have big trauma in your life to experience feelings and symptoms associated with trauma. I was the girl that had it all on paper, no big dramas to note, yet I had trauma responses in my body when triggered. This manifested in me frantically tidying up kids' toys while having palpitations – tidying was my go-to, to avoid feeling!

I have learnt to be in my body, and before my nervous system gets over-stimulated, I slow down and nurture myself instead of pushing myself to the limit, which previously would have ended up with a 'need' for a glass or two of wine, or over-eating to avoid feeling. Where are you over-stimulating your nervous system and burying the feelings that need to come up for release? Are you over-working or busying yourself to avoid the unpleasant feelings from the past? Is your nervous system on alert and needs a glass of wine to calm it? Come on, be honest with yourself. You know you are doing it. I was on course for adrenal fatigue – a common ailment in today's go go go society. But it doesn't have to be that way. I am now so much slower with my day and I don't mean in efficiency but in the energy I allow to flow through my nervous system.

It's time to calm your system, feel your body and respond to its needs and I don't mean in the wine sense! I recently had a client come to me feeling stuck and overwhelmed with life as a mum. I could literally feel her heightened energy coursing through her body. When we began the session, it turns out she was a people pleaser and found it hard to say no, to the detriment of her health. She had also found that being 'busy' stopped her from feeling her feelings and connecting with her children on a deep level. She was running her busy mum's pattern and didn't know it until I showed her. Are you using being busy as a way to avoid feeling or looking at the past? If so, it's time to unbusy yourself. How does this look? Delegate, delegate, delegate, stop being a martyr and delegate! You don't have to do it all or be it all. You are enough just as you are and you need to slow down, get in to your body and relax. I use meditation and yoga as a wonderful tool to connect with my inner self, and a time I remember to breathe from a conscious place. It sounds ridiculous but we forget to breathe and this is what keeps us alive. I never truly understood the benefits of yoga or meditation until I began to do it and then found that it became my place of sanctuary and calm. There are many ways to mediate, there is no right or wrong as long as you are slowing down your thoughts. It's the same with yoga – pick a type that works for you. I love Yin yoga as it is so restful and calming.

Did you know that way back when, women lived in tribes and this is how they managed bringing up children, running the home and keeping the ship afloat. Whether you have kids or not, or a business, or run a home, we must all have a tribe of people around us to help us keep afloat so that when you're struck down with a cold, period pains or fatigue, you have a group of women to help you. Modern life has cut us off from this tribal feel but it is essential to a woman's sense of self, ability to grow and to feel safe. This might not come in the form of a parent or siblings but great if it does. If not, you can create a tribe around you. Remember you attract according to your vibe, so set an intention to form a tribe around you and before you know it, they'll arrive one by one. I went from having a cleaner a couple of times a week prior kids; nowadays, I have a whole tribe around me including a cleaner, babysitters who share my same values and methods, a coach for my blind spots (yep, I still have them!) and of course my dear girlfriends – many of whom I have made following my journey back to me. Recruit the free and willing support of those close and dear to you to help you through life, it doesn't have to cost. You'll be amazed what help there is out there.

Don't do life alone anymore, reach out and make loneliness a thing of the past. If you are connected with yourself, your inner child, you're meeting your needs and have a tribe of support – what more could you ask for?

Do you know the power of women together? Neither did I until I began spending more time in women's circles. Yep, you heard me! Last year I spent a week in the depths of the countryside surrounded by 14 wonderful women. I have connected with a part of life I didn't know existed in this form. The first night we came in all modern womanly, defensive, not sharing, closed. Slowly but surely, deep into the earth I went, deep into the earth I now know. We came together. I held hands with sisters and journeyed deep into a part of me which activated my inner strength and a realisation that women want to support and care for each other, contrary to what society is brainwashing us to think.

For six days I did yoga outside, sitting around in circles singing, dancing, crying and letting go – and surrounded by goats. At the start of the week, I knew none of the women; by the end, we were soul sisters or, as I like to put it, Shakti Sisters! A magical space is formed when women come together to heal. This is true connection, when vulnerability is shared, tears are held and honesty is revealed. It is true: women are strong and even stronger together. I can't recommend joining a women's circle enough, for the purpose of tuning in to your cyclical self, your inner wisdom and reconnecting with your ancestral power. Do not underestimate the power of high vibe unions with like-minded women – ditch the gossip, bin the judgements of others, just let go, allow, be open and bring your nurturing, feminine self to the table and you'll witness something infinitely magical. The power of the fem is second to none. You heard it here first.

PULL THE TRIGGER, I'M DONE

What does it really mean to be triggered? It is a moment or scenario that triggers your subconscious mind back to an old memory or feeling when your mind is transported to a time in your childhood where you felt not enough, frightened, powerless, hopeless or helpless; the list goes on. Although you might not recollect the memory during the triggering moment, your body remembers and as your mind recollects it sends a message to your body in the form of hormones and this manifests in physiological symptoms, such as anger which comes with heat in the body, palpitations in the chest, an increase of nervous energy. Prior to understanding your make up, you were permanently being triggered, without even noticing it because you don't know any different. The moments you reached for the wine, the fags, coffee and crappy food you were diluting the feelings that the trigger unlocked.

A good example of a trigger is when you have a to-do with your boss (let's make her female for now) and she asks to see your latest project to give you feedback. She reviews your work and proceeds to lay into you, criticising your ideas, blaming you for not being as across the work as she would like. The reality of this situation is, this was never really about you; maybe your work was under par, maybe not, but your boss is over-worked and feeling the pressure and projecting onto you. Because her reaction was an 'over-reaction', it is clear that she has been triggered as she isn't handling this like an adult but probably like an angry, overwhelmed teenager. Had she been coming from a functional place, she would have delivered her feedback in a healthy, compassionate and constructive way but as she was triggered she didn't. This then led you to be triggered back to memories of a female criticising and diminishing your creativity and work which later manifested in a belief of 'I'm not enough'. She triggered that belief and you walked away from that meeting feeling very not enough. Remember this isn't about the present, this was about the past and a female (maybe mum or a critical teacher) acting in a similar manner that triggered the emotional response within you.

How to remedy a trigger? Simple. Inner. Child. Work. That little girl in you needs to know that first, she is enough and that it's okay to make mistakes, she isn't meant to be perfect, far from it. Life is about learning and there is a gift in everything. That boss, like her or not, is a gift. Why? Because she has taken you back to an event that needed healing. If you don't go back and do the work with your inner child, more people like your boss are going to turn up in your life until you get the message and do the inner work.

SUPERWOMAN AT WORK

Another key tool that I have used on myself and share with my clients is visualising your Superwoman rescue. When you have been triggered and you can feel feelings coming up that feel uncomfortable, take some time to sit with them and allow them to come up. This isn't always possible if you are at work and it's manic but in those situations I take myself off to the toilet – no one can object to you nipping off to the bog! Sit down, breathe and connect with that part of you that has been triggered. Bring forward your little girl in your mind and open up a dialogue with her. Ask how she is feeling and what that situation made her feel. She will no doubt say that the person in the incident reminded her of someone from the past, when they disempowered her, made her feel small, insignificant, not enough. You need to remind her that this is different now, tell her you're sorry she felt like that and that she no longer needs to worry as you are here to keep her safe.

Here's the juicy bit. Now bring forward the memory of when she felt disempowered, see the place that it took place – recreate the whole place in your mind as you review the incident from the past. As the incident unfolds, I want you to enter the scene as a functional adult and rescue your little girl. Pick her up, boundary the perpetrators on her behalf and take her out of the situation. In essence, you are rewriting the scene and your brain does not know if it is real or false – you are literally rewriting the past so that when another situation takes place with such triggers, your memory of the event will be your new one. Keep doing this until the body and mind are aligned, every single time this occurs the emotional charge in your body will become less and less until it is no longer there and the trigger is defused. If you do the work, you truly can change your life and how you respond to life's unfoldings. It's just knowing what to do in the given situations and how to change and this is what I give you.

YOU ARE THE FIRE

What are you angry about? Come on, be honest. It's not the mess in your kid's room or your boyfriend's antics, it's not your boss or your colleagues getting up your nose, it's not even your mate who hasn't replied to your text – it's way deeper than that. You can keep projecting it on the present and convince yourself it is, but hear this right now, it's not – it's an old feeling from the past that you are making about the present. Of course, your husband or partner might have crossed a boundary and done something that you disagree with but if you're not triggered by it you wouldn't be angry, you would be functional, balanced and be able to respond as opposed to react. I know you don't want to hear this but it's true. It took me a while to grasp this concept and I did truly believe that it was about the present, not the past, but I later learnt otherwise.

Your inner child knows what you're angry about – most likely the teenage part of you, they love to be cross and grumpy at life! Are you behaving in a teenage manner, all bolshie and cross?

As you read this, are you thinking, 'I'm not an angry person, I never get angry, no, not me'? Yep, I thought that too. Before I had children, it took a lot, and I mean A LOT, to push my buttons. I vividly remember my first outburst. It was when I was pregnant with my first child and my husband came in blind drunk and while I helped him down the stairs he called me a w*nker! I mean, of all things! Well, that was it, by the fourth time he said it, I flipped out. 'How dare you called the mother of your future child such a thing!' That was the start of my bubbling anger that eventually came out like a volcano when I finally gave birth to my son and my future self for that matter. (Don't worry, I forgave him and he hasn't called me that again!) I don't mean I was angry when I physically gave birth, I mean when I would stub my toe running to change my baby's nappy or when I dropped the organic carrot puree on the floor. All of these little things were being sent to me to bring my deep anger up. I wasn't really angry about the carrot puree. Eventually after a couple of years of this, I realised that this wasn't me. I didn't want to be angry anymore and I didn't want to suppress it any longer. You see, I had played Little Miss Perfect as a child and she does not get angry. I had learnt that it wasn't safe to show my anger, there was no space in my family home to be angry – that was left to Dad and my brothers. There I was containing it, swallowing it, eating it until thirty-odd years later when – puke, it all came up. Was it safe for you to be angry as a child? Was there space for you to feel this and let it out? Remember emotions are energy and they need to move, it needs to travel out of the body otherwise we store it inside and it comes out in your car, when someone cuts you up.

As mentioned, one likes to wear rose-tinted glasses and avoid acknowledging that our parents annoyed us as children. By holding this anger in due to shame of letting it out, it gets stuck in us but it's okay to admit they let you down and didn't meet your needs. It's absolutely fine to openly say (not to their face mind!) that you resent your siblings being born because life changed and so did the level of attention your parents gave you. It's okay to admit these things because when we do, we get it out, we feel the feelings and then let them go so there is no emotional charge behind the thoughts. Then you can remedy the old feelings of resentment and productively reframe them because the chances are you have told yourself a very tall story as a kid and this was never about you.

One of the safest ways to release anger and make way for lurve (love), one that I used many a time, is listening to a guided meditation on anger release when you are triggered so that you go straight to the past rather than react disproportionally in the present. While listening to one of these, you can let it out, shout it out (on your own in a room where you won't be disturbed) or you can just see the old scene in your head and imagine saying everything you need to say to the person who needs to hear it. You can also release anger by punching pillows, twisting a towel, boxing, running – whatever way it allows you to feel the energy rise in your body for release and set your intention to let go of the anger that is no longer serving you. This anger needs to be heard and set free so that you can set yourself free and when you do this in a safe and controlled environment no one else gets hurt with words and you get the chance to release.

I'M NOTTT ANGRY!!!!!! OK?!

Darling, honestly you can keep telling yourself you're not but you are. I can feel it. Historically, it's not been safe for women to feel and show their anger – we're labelled crazy, over-emotional or out of control. Well, we aren't. We have a wild side and a part of us that feels so deeply, openly with all our soul to bare. This is the gift of being a woman, it's our feminine traits that are within us. We are here to nurture, feel and comfort. In order to efficiently do our job at helping others you must help yourself first and understand your emotions so that you can navigate them in a loving and compassionate way and then - and only then - can you help others to do the same. Lead by example.

So, let's raise your vibration, raise the vibration of the collective consciousness and let this sh*t go. Whoever you are angry at, whatever it might be, it's okay. Don't project. Own it. Acknowledge it. Allow it to come up and then let it go.

LET IT GO

Just like Elsa did in Frozen, it's time to let the sh*t go. Whether that comes in the form of releasing your anger in a safe and healthy environment or writing a letter to the person who hurt you (don't send it though, it's just a form of release), filling your journal, exercising with an intention to release, as long as you are letting go of the stored feelings and memories, unleashing the sadness, pain, fear, resentment, shame, guilt it has to come out. Writing things down is a powerful way to release what is in our minds. One of the ways I love to let go is in a women's circle, around a fire, surrounded with love and support. This is such a powerful way to safely, while being held, let go of the old and invite the new. Moon gatherings are becoming more and more common in the modern world as we turn back to ancient rituals that brought great healing. What are you ready to let go of? What part of you no longer serves you? What pattern of behaviour, what repetitive thought are you sick of? You're no victim, sweetheart, you have control of your life and if you're ready you can change the way you think, live and love. It starts today.

CRY BABY CRY

'No one ever died of crying' – words by Marisa Peer[5] – and it's true. Tears are you just watering your soul. Crying is one of the greatest, most wonderful ways to release yet we shame it

---

[5]   Copyright Marisa Peer

and apologise for it. It's okay to cry in fact, tears are the most healings waters on Earth. It is a spontaneous way to release emotions and it not only heals and clears your mind but also your body. When we cry the tears release stress hormones that have built up in the body. On top of this, tears are 95% anti-bacterial, when we cry we lubricate the eye, and the list goes on. What if you don't? Your stress levels will rise and your emotions will bubble out in another form or just get trapped in your body. Either way, it isn't pretty. So, get those tissues out, put on an old mix tape or whack on a tear-jerking movie; however you need to let the tears out, do it. We always feel better after a cry because we have made room, let go of stored repressed and suppressed emotions.

What if I never cry? Well, darling, something or someone has given you a belief that it's not safe to share your feelings, that you can't be vulnerable. It's time to work on that because there is pain there, big or small, and it needs to come out. We all need a good old cry, especially those ones with the repetitive inhalations where you can barely catch your breath, yeah those ones! So, no more apologising, feeling ashamed of shedding a tear – after all, tears are words the heart can't say. Tears are not a sign of weakness, they are a sign of courage to be vulnerable, to show your heart, your soul, your truth. Simply put, when you hold back tears, you are drowning your heart. Let it sing, let it out, let you be free. Bare your soul, be brave while being vulnerable and most importantly, let it flow.

HAPPINESS IS ACCEPTANCE

Time does not heal everything but acceptance heals everything. After you let go of intense emotions, unburden your past and water your soul with tears, you make so much space in your life for love, joy and passion – of course, that is if you have truly resolved and reconciled your old stories and the root of your beliefs. Have you found peace with the old story? Have you finally accepted that, yes it was hard at times, your parents didn't meet all your needs (if any), yes you once felt not enough because of X, Y or Z? Have you really let go of the emotions behind it so that you can sit in peace with it and call it your old story, the old.........*insert your name here*............story? I like to refer to my life in two parts – Old Cat (I don't mean in age terms!! I mean pre-forty, former Cat) and New Cat. Without acknowledgement and then acceptance, how can you really and truly feel happiness? This isn't about forgiving, even though that's wonderful too and comes alongside acceptance. It's about simply and finally accepting the old story for what it was. You can't change it but you can change how you move forward. It's time to see the flaws in the other person(s) that caused you pain/feelings of inadequacy, de-pedestal them and know that they behaved like they did, not because you did anything wrong, but that they had their stuff going on. Life was as it was and there is a great gift in that, even though you might not see it at first. You have learnt and endured a valuable life lesson, it just came in a shitty package. As I look back over my past, I can see how it was perfectly manicured and delivered to create my purpose – what I do now. I'm deeply and truly grateful for my not-so-perfect childhood because if I hadn't experienced what I had then, I wouldn't be doing what I do now, and this is what makes my heart sing and dance, rock and roll and backflip three times over. As I look back, everything that I deemed bad or a mistake has shaped me and given me tools to live my purpose. Everything has unfolded exactly the same way for you. Everything is just as it should be. The Universe never makes mistakes and your path to date is absolutely as it's needed to be. Don't doubt that for a minute. Look for the gift, there's one lurking in there somewhere, you've just got to look a little harder.

What have I discovered?

What do I want to change?

What do I want to create?

☆

'Don't die with *glitter*

still in your bones.'

Your

Powerful

Mind

step two - change
chapter four

Darling,

Have you seen the headlines, read the magazines, the papers, all the books?

Now is the time to rise up, to show up and own your feminine power and be you.

The world needs your sparkle right now.

Wakey wakey, sweetheart!

Shine on, Sister!

Love,

Your Self-Esteem

'You didn't wake up today to be mediocre,
you woke up today and realised you are the
absolute bomb!'

Anonymous quote reinterpreted by Me.

Self-limiting beliefs nailed, purge complete, what next? Mind control. I don't mean in the weird sense but once you have understood your past and felt the feelings you can really begin to play and learn how to keep charge of that naughty thing called your mind. Some refer to it as your monkey mind and I'm going to teach you how to become the master of that cheeky monkey so that when it plays up, you know exactly what to do.

I acquired much of my knowledge about the brain and how it works from world-renowned hypnotherapist and psychologist Marisa Peer when I trained as a hypnotherapist. I learnt the trade after doing the personal work on myself with my coach. I learnt the tools to transcend my thoughts, beliefs and actions of habit by understanding how our hugely powerful brain works. Sounds complex, I know, but if you can learn the basics of this and why it works then you are the master of your life.

STAYIN' ALIVE

First key thing to know about your mind is that it is programmed to keep you alive at all costs,[6] no matter what; its motive, aim, instinct is to make sure beautiful and wonderful you stays safe and on this planet. It will do whatever it has to do to ensure this. Your brain finds what causes pain and keeps you away from it. Little has changed since early human brains lived on the planet: the brain is a survival organ and is designed to solve problems related to surviving in an unstable outdoor environment, to avoid danger and stay safe. Your brain still runs on this very principle, it looks for any sort of danger and stays clear of it. It does this by actively seeking out anything that has caused it any sort of pain, or fight or flight response in the body. Whether it's a bumble bee that once stung you on the leg or a type of food that once caused you to be ill, the brain sees it as danger. With that in mind, in early childhood, if you encountered a situation where you almost drowned in a pool, the next time you are in a similar scenario or go near to a pool, your mind will go into the fight or flight mode. As a consequence, it will do everything it can to ensure you don't go near the water again and will create a phobia response and this will continue into adulthood until it is addressed and healed. This is your subconscious moving you away from pain (danger) and towards pleasure (safety). Pain comes in many forms, it isn't just pain in the literal sense. Pain can be letting go of a friend who has hurt you,

---

[6]   Copyright Marisa Peer

stopping you from eating chicken because it has made you ill once, fear of dogs because once you were bitten by one, phobia of the dark because you may have experienced a scary moment that was in the dark.

If you are feeling resistance to letting go of old beliefs, sabotaging your route to greatness, procrastinating about embarking on a new business or perhaps avoiding making the first step towards your dream, then this is because your mind is responding to what it thinks you want. It is keeping you away from the painful thing that it thinks will take place if you don't do any of the above sabotage-type of things. Underneath your conscious desires, your subconscious mind is holding onto memories and beliefs that do not align with your conscious plans and therefore it blocks you. This can be incredibly frustrating and equally puzzling as your conscious mind is game on for smashing the glass ceiling, but the 'computer' (your mind) says 'no'.

Little did I know as a 25-year-old how my subconscious was working to hold me back, or rather keep me safe. With a big desire to be loved, seen and appreciated, it was no surprise that I had a desire to be an actress (just like Mum). It is quite a common profession to fall into if you have suffered with a lack of being celebrated, acknowledged and adored – the stage is the perfect setting to put on a mask and be applauded by an audience to fulfil needs of being wanted, seen and heard. I had big dreams as a child of being (shining) on stage, being the lead role in a musical or play. I longed for the spotlight (at home and as a future profession). The trouble was that underneath all of this, I had limiting beliefs of it not being 'safe' to shine. This belief was formed in my family dynamic and my subconscious mind did everything it could to sabotage and block me from shining and 'taking the stage'. This manifested in anxiety that would take over and affect my interviews for jobs (and therefore I didn't get the gig). This came in the form of incessant stumbling reading the autocue at my Sky Sports screen test, tripping over my tongue when I presented at Chelsea TV. Quite simply, my subconscious programming was not in the game for shining or helping me get there, it was purely in the place of f*cking it up royally! That said, as I look back, everything was perfectly aligned to get me here today. Cheers to my subconscious mind because it thinks it's keeping me 'safe' but as it's acting on outdated beliefs, it's no longer doing the job it thinks it is but it can't let go of the belief until I actively understand and choose to let go of it and change my beliefs.

The next key thing to know about humans is, we are programmed to seek connection and avoid rejection at all costs.[7] We thrive when we are connected, in a group, surrounded by like-minded people. Whether connection exists in a relationship, friendship, the bond with our parents and family – humans love to feel connection and will do their utmost to avoid any sort of disconnection. With this in mind, we humans will do anything to feel that connection,

---

[7] Copyright Marisa Peer

which often means twisting oneself into a pretzel and going against our values just to feel accepted. This can manifest in people pleasing, putting other people's needs before yours or even saying and being an altered version of yourself. This often leads us to being somewhat disloyal to our true selves because we end up not meeting our needs, not listening to what is best for us and our health and emotional well-being. It's rather like fashion, we follow the trends, not just because we like the particular item in favour but also to feel part of something, to feel like others, connected, accepted – if I dress the same as others, I will avoid being rejected. Or perhaps you eat and drink things that your best or true self doesn't really like? I know I love red wine; as a twenty-something I found a glass of red at the table with my Dad gave me connection to him. I still enjoy red wine but I enjoy it from a conscious place rather than drinking it to fill that void of disconnection. Where have you gone against your truth just to feel connected? Whose needs are you putting first? Are you speaking your truth or hiding it for fear of disconnection?

Another key thing I learnt when training as a hypnotherapist was how the mind and body work. All too often, the mind and body are treated as separate entities; yet they aren't – they are intrinsically linked and this is how I saw it for my own eyes.

☆ IN THE SPOTLIGHT ☆
LET'S GET ALL ZESTY [8]

Close your eyes (don't worry, I'm not going to get you to do anything silly). I want you to imagine a juicy, bright yellow, zesty lemon in your hands. Imagine that you just picked it straight off the tree. You're really thirsty and longing for something to quench your thirst. Feel the lemon in your hand, the pitted, waxy skin. Now think about raising the lemon up to your nose. Smell it, breathe in all that lemony, fresh, gorgeous scent, really let it in and enjoy that cleansing smell. Next I want you to imagine taking an enormous bite of the lemon – you can taste the sour, bitter, strong lemon taste. Swirl it around your mouth, squeeze more juice in to your mouth.

I bet your face is a picture as you visualised this. Now hands up whose mouth filled up with saliva as you carried out that short visualisation.[8]

This is a simple illustration of how the body responds to the images that you give it. The image of the lemon evoked a chemical reaction in the body which caused the production of saliva in the mouth. Now go back to the concept that everything is energy and each thought or feeling has its own frequency and consequently vibrates at a certain rate. If you keep talking to yourself in a negative way, your body has a chemical and hormonal reaction in the body. Depending on the nature and frequency of the words used, the reaction will be of the same vibration. The fact is, you can choose

---

[8]   Copyright Marisa Peer

the words or images you give your mind but you cannot choose the reaction, whether that is disease in the body or manifesting low vibration outcomes. With this in mind, you can see why it is vitally important to use positive words and phrases when talking to ourselves and, of course, others.

TO BE OR NOT TO BE?

Did you know that your mind doesn't know what is real and what is fake? When you watch television, your mind thinks what it is watching is real. It cannot differentiate between the two. If you are someone who enjoys watching horror movies, nail-biting thrillers or even depressing and dramatic EastEnders (one of the UK's favourite soap operas) be mindful because when you feel the feelings of fear (although they aren't real) your body's response is the same as if it was. It is crucial to fill it with high vibe television fodder, inspiring and educational movies and documentaries, material to grow your mind and evoke positive hormones and chemical reactions in your body. Imagine if you watched fear-mongering television often, think how highly stressed or even anxious your mind and body would be? Imagine what a strain that would be on your nervous system! Quit the low vibe four-eyes stuff and let's get high end.

YOU ARE NOT WHO YOU THINK YOU ARE

One of the most eye-opening concepts (third eye, even – the gateway to your intuition, creativity and superpowers) that I discovered as I read more and more about the mind was the idea that we are pure consciousness. When we are born onto this planet, society tells us our name, gender, age, religion, nationality, job title. It tells us what we should wear, how we must act, what we must do to live a happy life. Society also teaches us that we are our possessions. If I own a Ferrari, I will be happy. If I have a big house, I am successful. On top of this, we are taught that we are our thoughts. We are led to believe we are our thoughts, our mind, our body, our smell, our looks. Well, truth bomb about to drop. We are none of these things, we are far more magical than any of those labels.

If you discovered in Step 1 that you have held self-limiting beliefs such as, 'I'm not enough as I am, I'm not lovable or success is unavailable to me' and then you believe that you are those thoughts, I have this to tell you: you are not. You are separate from your thoughts. You are not even your mind. Your thoughts are there to be changed and they are also there to be let go of. Imagine if you understood that your thoughts are not yours and you allow the thoughts (good and bad) to just flow, come in to your head and leave as quickly as they came, without any story around the thought. You see, we are our own worst enemy because when a thought comes into our head we attach to it and put a whole, whopping story around it. Let me explain further. Imagine this: You are due to meet a friend but they are late. Lately she has been a bit absent-minded and preoccupied with her life and rather grumpy. When half an hour passes, you have wrapped a big story around why she hasn't turned up. 'She is so selfish, she is so annoying, she never texts anymore and lets me know. I think she must be in a mood with me because I couldn't chat to her on the phone the other day while I was putting the kids to bed. Oh no, maybe something has happened to her? Or have I done something to upset her? Oh goodness, did I get the wrong week? Oh gosh, I'm so not enough, I feel shit. I thought all those things about her and actually I messed up and got the date wrong...bla bla bla bla...' A whole load of non-verbal mental diarrhoea ensued all because you got attached to the thought. Yes, your mate didn't turn up but you needn't put that whole load of drivel around the reason she didn't turn up. You then walked away from the situation feeling overwhelmingly not enough. You triggered the non-happy hormones in your body and agreed that you are in actual fact, not enough. STOP RIGHT THERE, THANK YOU VERY MUCH – as the Spice Girls once sang – why did you need to agree with your thoughts just then? How many times have you done that? Just because your mind has chosen to tell you that you aren't enough, you don't have to go along with it! If it told you to jump off a cliff, would you? No, exactly! So why do you need to go along with its outdated and crappy labels it has given you? So what you gonna do about it? Change them, that's right, and not get attached to the thoughts in the first place! Liberating, I know! Thoughts, beliefs and old stories are there to be changed and challenged. You are in control of your life, not the other way around. Your mind doesn't run the show (well, currently it might but we are working on that now) – you do.

If we go further, Eckhart Tolle, the master of mindfulness and spirituality, says that you aren't your mood either. Well, that's a relief. You are not grumpy. Great. That's that then. Move on. No. Wait a minute. He states, 'If there is unhappiness in you, first you need to acknowledge that it is there. But don't say, "I am unhappy". Unhappiness has nothing to do with who you are. Say, "there is unhappiness in me". Then investigate it.'

By using the words 'I am' you are claiming ownership of this. Where else do you own labels that either you gave yourself or that others have given you in the past? Are you ready to detach from your moods and instead change the way your view a mood that unfolds with a sense of curiosity? Are you ready to detach from old labels? Let me go further and guide you to how you might do this. You wake up one morning feeling irritable and you can hear your mind chatter going and it goes something like this *'Ugh I'm so annoyed, I've got to do the washing before I go to work. Ouch I just tripped over my shoes, bloody boyfriend left them there. Ugh he is so annoying. Right, cup of tea will help. F*ck I just burnt my hand – arrrrghhh. This is a sh*t start to the day. I'm going back to bed.'* How about you changed that and observed the mood that has come up with a sense of curiosity, *'oh that's interesting I'm feeling irritable, I'm just going to sit with that feeling, something has triggered this in me, breathe through it and let it go.'* This way there is no attachment, the mood is not yours, there's no ownership. Avoid going in to a deep analysis of what went on for you, chances are you know already what was behind the irritability and can dialogue with your inner child and put her mind at ease that she is safe and loved and all will be well.

To top this off, Eckhart (I'm going on a first-name basis after quoting him once already!) says that we also aren't our bodies! He states that you are pure consciousness, residing in a thing called a body during your time on planet Earth. I know, deep stuff and I won't blow your mind too much as I have already thrown some big science truths out there which you might still be computing. It's true though, Deepak Chopra explains it brilliantly, 'You are not merely the physical that you identify with out of habit. Your essential state is a field of infinite possibilities.' That said, we are pure consciousness hosted in a temporal body and mind, living an experience on this planet. So, the less attachment to this form, the better. I'm off on a metaphysical tangent, someone stopppp meee! I'm back. Right, point is, we must allow the flow of life through our minds and bodies, allow the experiences to unfold and come out of big stories and unnecessary noise in our minds. Open your mind and stop living in this insular view of what or who you are because you are so much more than this. When you tune in to the mind's capabilities and consequently yours, you open your life to magic that awaits. If you are pure consciousness with infinite possibilities, what does the future hold for you? Ahh, that's why we need to work on your mind so it's creating an infinitely happy, joy-filled life that you have manifested yourself because you understand how capable and brilliant you are. Your mind is the vehicle to your greatness: you can drive it towards your dreams or let it rust away in the dusty garage of lost hopes and missed chances. I know what I choose, how about you?

EAT. SLEEP. DRINK. REPEAT.

Another key thing to remember is, our minds learn through repetition.[9] If we keep telling ourselves that we are useless, it will learn it pretty quickly. A baby practises and practises a new skill until the brain and muscle memory is formed. If you brainwash yourself with words of greatness, it will learn greatness pretty quickly. Practice makes perfect (or near enough). What do you choose to repeatedly fill your mind with? I go with positivity and high vibe words and phrases to overhaul the old programming by whatever means necessary, hypnosis, guided meditation, affirmations – you name it, I do it. Over and over I reminded myself, even as far as to say 'indoctrinated' myself with words and images of enoughness so that my mind had no choice but to take them on. I even use my social media to affirm the positive things I feel about myself – I follow inspiring accounts that repeatedly confirm

---

[9]   Copyright Marisa Peer

the mindset I choose to take on. Eventually the new beliefs became mine and I don't mean in the ownership terms but as the thoughts drifted in, instead of them being negative and taking hold of them, they would be positive and I would observe them and then let them go.

WORK IT BABY

Now you've chosen to vibe high and you have aligned your thoughts, you're going to repeat them over and over, without getting attached to them or your body! You're learning fast! Want some more? Good.

Did you know, the brain is a muscle that needs to be worked? Yep, just like you're repeating a positive affirmation over and over, it's like your brain is being exercised, and as we all know, our bodies like to be exercised and 'run' on a daily basis to get the blood flowing, energy coursing through your body, chi fully charged, shakti on full power, prana running on high. How do you choose to exercise your mind in order to achieve the mindset you desire? Meditation, hypnosis, guided meditations? In the next chapter, I go into why these methods work and what effects they have on the brain, but for now, start to get used to the idea that a daily practice is something that you will need to adopt in order to change the way you think, live and love. I have had numerous people come to me expecting to change their life in one session. Now don't get me wrong, so much can be achieved in one session and I have many people who walk out after a single session feeling very different, understanding their old programming and with a load of healing under their belt. But while this is amazing, you must commit to listening to a recording or such like (a guided meditation or hypnosis that uses positive empowerment to replace old limiting beliefs), and consciously making an effort to change the old habits of thought and also commit to changing your life so that when you are faced with a choice of playing out the old pattern or choosing a new path, you consciously make the right choice in line with who you are choosing to become.

I have said it before and I will say it again, beliefs are there to be changed and upgraded. If you don't, you'll stay where you are. Challenge them, challenge yourself and change your trajectory. As kids, we created beliefs that eventually became us and we became a walking, talking embodiment of this belief, carrying out choices, actions and habits that are in line with those thoughts and beliefs. Eventually these early beliefs became your life. If only you had known this as a little girl, things could have been so different. But it's never too late to change your life or your mind. As you create new beliefs, the beliefs become your new habits, choices, feelings, actions and thoughts. What do you believe? Do you believe in yourself? I believe in you. Let's start creating the change within you.

CHANGE NOTHING AND NOTHING CHANGES

True that! Change is often met with fear, fear of the unfamiliar, fear of failure, fear of what might lie ahead.

Truth is, the mind wants to grow, it wants to experience new sensations, new places, new people, new hobbies or skills. It's back to that need to exercise your brain, exercise and grow it, open it up to new concepts and ways life can be. Who wants to stay stuck? Not you! You want more from life and with that comes change.

As this Step is all about creating the change within you, it all comes down to choices. Are you choosing to change, to do the work on yourself so that you can embark on Step 3 and create a life you want and dream of? Let go of fear (it's an illusion), let in change, transformation and open yourself up to the flow of life and the growth of you. We are a result of all the choices we have made, big and small throughout our lives. If we have an old story running in our head that we are inadequate, then the choices we have made will have validated this. Choose a different story and make better choices and your life will change. Tony Robbins, leading author and philanthropist, talks about how leaders make decisions: it's because they are decisive and they are clear on what they want and why. 'When it comes to making decisions, be clear about what you really want—and why you want it. You've got to get absolutely crystal clear about your outcome and your purpose. If you forget the reasons behind your decision, you won't follow through.'

I got crystal clear on what I wanted and I chose to change my life because the old model wasn't working and in doing so, I will rest in peace knowing I pushed myself, smashed goals, experienced true happiness, allowed creativity to flood out of me like a tsunami and fulfilled my life purpose on this planet. How about that for life goals? You too can do this when you commit to change. When you make the choice to invest in yourself and your life. You have so much to give darling, don't die with glitter still in your bones. Unleash your inner sparkle. Change is good. Transformation of yourself is even better.

Let the change begin. (This is getting exciting!)

What have I discovered?

What do I want to change?

What do I want to create?

'It's time to really live.
Sparkle hard.'

Your Toolbox to Greatness

chapter five

Darling,

A word in your ear...

That little girl inside of you has a message for the world – don't silence her any longer.

Let her shout from the rooftops, shine her light and share her message.

Speak out, I'm listening. Always.

Your voice matters, every word of it.

Shine on, Sister!

Love

Your Self-Esteem

'She was powerful not because she wasn't scared but because she woke up and faced her fears with courage written across her heart.'

An anonymous quote reinterpreted by Me

It's a myth that the mind is complex.[10] Of course, it is an immensely powerful organ with infinite capabilities but the key rules of your mind are simple and give you great freedom over your life. In order for you to understand how to heal your self-esteem, it is important that I show you how and, mostly importantly, why the mind tools I share with you in this book work.

You now know that the key thing to know about your amazingly powerful brain is that its number one responsibility is to keep you alive at all costs and your mind believes whatever you tell it.[11] If you keep telling it 'I can't, I can't do this', your mind responds and the outcome is, wait for it... 'you can't'. If, on the other hand, you tell it 'I can, this is easy, I can do this effortlessly', then your mind will follow. Your mind needs clear instructions in line with your goals otherwise it will play havoc if you don't take control of it. Your mind is like a classroom full of naughty schoolchildren who, until the teacher comes in and instructs them, will run riot. In this chapter, you are going to

---

[10] [11] Copyright Marisa Peer

learn about how the mind works so that you can take back the power and transform your life so that it matches what you want as opposed to what you don't want! Once you know these tools, you can dialogue with your mind and you can be in charge, you rather your deep-rooted outdated programming!

YOUR SUBCONSCIOUS MIND

Let me introduce you to your subconscious mind – the storage room of everything that is currently not in your conscious mind. The subconscious mind stores all of your life experiences, beliefs, memories, skills, plus all situations you've been through as well as all images you've ever seen – even if you can't remember them, they're all there. Now that's quite something, isn't it? Your conscious mind commands and your subconscious mind obeys, it's like an eager friend that works tirelessly 24 hours a day to make your behaviour fit a pattern consistent with your thoughts, hopes, and desires in your subconscious. In many ways your subconscious mind is like your best friend because it wants to please you in any way it can; but at the same time, it can be your own worst enemy if your subconscious beliefs hold you back from your conscious wants and desires – this is why it is key to aligning both, ensuring they want the same goals.

Caution: Do not underestimate the power of your subconscious mind, it is running the show!

If at an early age in your life you picked up beliefs that you are not enough, not lovable and don't matter, you will still be playing out these beliefs as an adult until you access them and let them go. This is why you have to take charge of it! Not only this, you will continue to be triggered by these emotions. The subconscious mind is responsible for the automatically triggered feelings and emotions that you suddenly experience when facing a new situation. For example, if you once gave a presentation that you forgot all your notes for and it went terribly, the next time you step up to public speak your mind gets triggered back to the scenario years before where you felt feelings of embarrassment and shame because you fluffed the presentation without your notes. Therefore the fear and anxiety feelings you feel the second time around are triggered by your subconscious recollection of a similar scenario years before. It matches any new scenario, situation or feeling with the old programming. And, as a consequence, your body launches into fear because it has recognised the situation and matched it to the one you encountered years before.

Your subconscious is like a huge memory bank and its capacity is virtually unlimited. Remember, it permanently stores everything that has ever happened to you. Listen to this for a statistic: by the time you reach the age of 21, you've already permanently stored more than one hundred times the contents of the entire Encyclopaedia Britannica. With that said, every emotion, both good and bad, from your childhood gets logged, which is why as an adult you might get an overwhelming feeling of happiness when you are on the beach, waves crashing, sandcastles being constructed, because your mind has transported you back to the feelings of happiness you will have experienced as a child on the beach. Equally, when someone shouts aggressively at you it might trigger a feeling of fear, regressing you back to the feelings you had when being shouted at by an abusive parent and reminding you of our powerlessness at that moment as a small child. I have often overheard mothers saying something about their child and how *'they will never remember, they're too young.'* WRONG!!! We remember it all, that's why being a parent or in a position of responsibility for a child, is such a great responsibility as you are predominantly responsible for your child's early programming. The function of your subconscious mind is to store and retrieve data. Its job is to ensure that you respond exactly the way you are programmed to. Therefore, it is hugely important to be conscious of your self-talk, the way in which you communicate with your conscious mind and your subconscious mind.

John Kehoe, a highly acclaimed author for his pioneering work in the field of mind power, describes the subconscious mind as a 'second, hidden mind that exists within you. It interprets and acts upon the predominating thoughts that reside within your conscious mind, and its goal is to attract circumstances and situations that match the images you have within'. In simple terms, you reap what you sow. He goes on to say that our subconscious mind is like 'a very fertile soil that will grow any seed you plant in it. Your habitual thoughts and beliefs are seeds that are being constantly sown. Just as corn kernels produce corn and wheat seeds produce wheat, the contents of your thoughts will have an effect in your life. You will reap what you sow; this is a law'. In short, your conscious mind is like the gardener who tends to the soil. It's up to you to choose wisely what reaches the 'inner garden' (your subconscious) and understand that is it your responsibility to tend to variety of seeds (good and bad) that have been planted. So, it's time to uproot the bad seeds that have become over-grown trees and plant some fresh ones so you can bloom and shine like a flower does.

THE GOOD NEWS

The good news is, you can re-programme your subconscious mind with various tools such as hypnosis, guided meditation and visualisations. When you access the subconscious mind, you can understand the root cause behind the early belief, when you have that information you can change the thought and consequently the habit of action. Why should you do this, I hear you ask?

Your beliefs become your thoughts, your thoughts become your words, your words become your actions, your actions become your habits, your habits become your values and your values become your destiny. Want to change your destiny? Then you need to go back and rewire your subconscious, replacing all your old, outdated beliefs with new, positive ones. Sounds exciting, doesn't it?

This is the fun part because you suddenly have the power and are no longer powerless to your circumstance. When I'm triggered by a situation (trust me, it still happens), because I understand how and where (Step 1) my limiting beliefs came from, I can step back and look at the thoughts and feelings coming up and recognise that they are old and no longer part of the new Cat that I have been working tirelessly on. I can then do the work (inner child or anger release most of the time) and then rewire my thoughts with either hypnosis, guided meditation or a meaty visualisation (such as the Superwoman rescue). Sounds simple and in essence it is, it just needs practice and focus.

LOOK IN TO MY EYES

There are various misconceptions about hypnosis. First, that it is all about looking into a crazy therapist's eyes while they dangle a pendulum in front of your face and then you will be 'under a spell' where you dance around doing silly things making a fool of yourself, like the famous Paul McKenna show on television some years back. The show was entertaining but far from how I practise hypnosis.

Hypnosis is simply a form of deep relaxation and involves the induction of a trance-like condition, much like when you are daydreaming and you go into autopilot. But when a client is in hypnosis, they are actually in an enhanced state of awareness, concentrating entirely on the therapist's voice. In this relaxed state, you bypass the critical mind and suppress the conscious mind (the voice you are more familiar with, that you hear in your head) while the subconscious mind is unlocked and you are able to access old memories and emotions. I like to think of hypnosis as the key to an old filing cabinet stuffed full of dusty old documents and information that you think you need in its entirety. When you get the key and open it, you can tidy it, throw out old stuff, keep the good stuff and then make way for more documents – fun ones, full of colour and inspiring words. Hypnosis has the ability to unlock stored emotions in the mind and this consequently makes way for good health – the clear mind equals a healthy body. Think of it as trapped energy being released, allowing a flow to return and harmony to be restored.

At the end of a hypnosis session with me (or any RTT therapist), you are given a recording to listen to so that you can embed the new-found knowledge and rewire your mind. When you listen to a hypnotic recording following a session with a therapist, it is important to listen to it for a minimum of 21 days as this is the time it takes to change a habit. This is essentially what happens when you practise something for that amount of time, your brain creates new neurological pathways and, hey presto, a new habit is formed. What habit, thought process or belief do you want to change? When you make the choice to change it, you can do it. Making your first step in that direction is the most powerful thing that you can do in order to become the person that you want to be.

When I trained as a hypnotherapist with Marisa Peer, she did a group hypnosis on building confidence and feeling 'enough'. I listened to it over and over any time that I was feeling 'not enough' and I swear to you, with no word of a lie, I began to believe it day by day and now I truly, with every cell of my body, believe it. It is my go-to phrase when there are moments of thinking 'oh, my hair doesn't look great or I don't know what to wear' – I remind myself, 'I am enough just the way I am.'

TALK IS CHEAP

It is my belief that it isn't enough to just talk about your past and expect it to be resolved; unless you go back and heal the past by letting go of the old emotions and change the way your subconscious is programmed, the pattern will continue to pop up. Naturally, a woman needs to talk about her feelings and a problem shared is indeed a problem halved but talking isn't enough to get to the root because your subconscious mind will do anything it can to avoid going to the root of the pain. You may manage to keep the undesirable habit at bay for a period of time, like when you're on a diet, but the subconscious mind and pattern kicks in and you enter into a sabotage pattern (on/off dieting). You have to change the thought AND habit of action. When you are under hypnosis, your mind likes to be told what to do; it has a willingness – the resistance comes down and you are open to positive suggestion.

I had a client who came to me after ten years of talk therapy, along with various other methods, but despite that she could not lift the feelings of worthlessness. Hypnosis was her last resort. When I regressed her, we got right to the core issue in the first 20 minutes of the session. It was all linked to her mother not having enough time for her and allocating more time with her younger sibling. This had led to feelings of inadequacy and a belief she wasn't lovable. Her early experiences as a child had shaped her future and at the age of 50, they were still running the same thought patterns, despite hours of talk therapy. It is important to get to the subconscious and uproot the memories so that you can reframe them, understand them and let them go.

THE MIND AND BODY LINK

Although it's important to re-programme the mind because it clears your mind and allows you to focus on the goals and dreams you had as a child before limiting beliefs were formed, it's also important to avoid disease in the body. As I have said, the word *disease* quite literally means *dis-ease*. Once you understand the power of your mind, you can go further and look at the mind-body link. The word psychosomatic refers to physical symptoms that occur for psychological reasons. Tears and blushing are examples of this, but they are normal responses that do not represent illness. It is only when psychosomatic symptoms go beyond the ordinary and impair your ability to function that illness results. It has been proven that if you are unwell and you adopt a positive mental attitude, you will have a better chance of recovery. Then there is the flip side, when people unconsciously think themselves ill. I have treated many clients with a condition or ill health as their main concern and once I regressed them under hypnosis, their subconscious mind showed them the events from their childhood that are the root cause and reason behind their current state of health. Clear the emotion behind the ailment or disease and sure enough, the ill health can repair. It feels like magic but really, it's just science or what is nowadays called neuroscience, science of the brain. If you can understand the way in which your brain works, alongside your own subconscious patterns of behaviour and the early memories and events that have shaped it, then you can go a long way in changing your internal chemistry. You are the placebo, you just need to activate it within. Your body and mind connection is more powerful than you can imagine. The first step is to be conscious of your behaviours and the events behind them. Your subconscious mind grows either flowers or weeds in the garden of your life; whichever you plant by the mental equivalents, you create. Choose your words carefully. Remember, you can choose the words you use but you can't choose the outcome and how it manifests in your mind or body. Words form the threads of how you live your life; your words become your reality.

Through the research of Dr Bruce Lipton and other leading-edge scientists, stunning new discoveries have been made about the interaction between our mind and body and the processes by which cells receive information. It shows that genes and DNA do not control our biology, that instead DNA is controlled by signals from outside the cell, including the energetic messages emanating from our thoughts. The new science of epigenetics is revolutionising our understanding of the link between mind and matter and the profound effects it has on our personal lives and the collective life of our species. This in turn can give you the power and allows you to control your environment, not just where you live but what you put in and on your body and the environment you live in emotionally. Toxic words can lead to a toxic body. Use the right language and it has been scientifically proven that good words create a big and positive effect on the body. Hypnotherapy and particularly the RTT method that I practise has phenomenal power to detox existing and out-of-date beliefs to allow for a new and up-to-date and healthy way of thinking. The power of your mind is so strong that you can instruct it to heal most ailments and disease. The power lies within you. There is no better time than now.

When you don't let go of emotions in a healthy way, they become stored in the body – I remember Marisa quoting the pioneering psychiatrist Henry Maudsley: 'The sorrow which finds no vent in tears, may make other organs weep' – cue ailments and disease. I see so many women who have suffered various health issues such as endometriosis, infertility, fibroids, irregular bleeding and, when under hypnosis, we found the conditions all originated from feelings of not enough, not worthy, and have manifested physically in the body.

I had a client who came to me desperate for help. Her health was at rock bottom and she was struggling with a long list of ailments including adrenal fatigue and a depleted immune system. She described her health as if her body was under constant attack. She had feelings of numbness, despair and a complete lack of self-worth. She was also suffering from agoraphobia. When we returned to the scenes under hypnosis, they were linked to the lack of security she felt as a child. She had a mentally ill mother who was always shouting and would wake her and her siblings up in the middle of the night with the doorbell. It would put her system on alert and she constantly felt unsafe. As a result of the lack of security she had experienced as a child, her body's natural defence (the immune system) was in overdrive, it had matched her thought process and was attempting to keep her safe. By creating a phobia of going outside, the mind thought that it was protecting her from people who in the past had harmed her. Once she could understand this link, we were able to calm both her nervous and immune systems and return her body to a sense of harmony and good health.

11 SHADES OF GREY MATTER: THE PRINCIPLES OF THE MIND

There are 11 key things to understanding your mind.[12] When I discovered them, it was not only fascinating but liberating to learn these simple but effective rules that allow you to understand why you think and behave like you do, because when you do you can get it working for you, not against you. Your mind is your friend, it just needs a helping hand. Understand these golden rules, and you're on a fast track to taking back control of your life and your mind

PRINCIPLE #1
YOUR WISH IS YOUR COMMAND

Your mind responds to everything you tell it and makes sure it's exactly what you want (even if that is linked to a deep subconscious thought). If you have formed early childhood beliefs such as 'I'm a failure' and you don't heal this or learn that you aren't and never were, you carry this through to adulthood. When you attempt to carry out an activity, new job or challenge, the subconscious programming is, 'I'm a failure' so your actions will align with this deep subconscious thought, even if your conscious mind is suggesting otherwise. I had an old programming similar to this linked to feeling inadequate: I never felt that I could achieve anything and

---

12   Copyright Marisa Peer

ended up quitting when the going got tough. I shouldered these feelings of inadequacy through my time in sport television and interior design, but it was only when I embarked on my transformation that I understood my programming and could let it go.

PRINCIPLE #2
CLOSE THE CURTAINS, YOU'VE GOT A NOSEY NEIGHBOUR

Your mind is like a chief curtain-twitcher – it's always watching (every single image you give it) and it's always listening (to every word you tell it). Words are far more powerful than the pictures you give it but both must be managed and regulated so that your mind doesn't respond. This is why the use of words to yourself and projection of pictures of yourself and your reality must be in line with the person that you want to be and become. This is important from a physiological perspective. In the book, *Words Can Change Your Brain* by Andrew Newberg, M.D. and Mark Robert Waldman, it is claimed: 'a single word has the power to influence the expression of genes that regulate physical and emotional stress.' Positive words, like peace and love, can alter the expression of genes. Simply put, words create chemical reactions in the body.

Let me enlighten you further: there was a study done by Masaru Emoto, a Japanese author and researcher who claimed that human consciousness (our thoughts) has an effect on the structure of water. He performed a series of experiments looking at the physical effect of words, prayers, music and environment on the crystalline structure of water (ice). He exposed the water to positive and negative words and music and found that the water that was exposed to positive words had completely symmetrical and perfectly formed ice particles. The water that had been exposed to negative words was disjointed and fractured throughout. Words such as 'love', 'truth' and 'peace' were all beautiful snowflake like crystalline structures under a microscope, whereas words such as 'evil', 'you disgust me' and 'you fool' were all deformed. Moreover, classical music had similar results to the positive words, while heavy metal was the opposite.

This proved with tangible evidence the power of the words and thoughts that come out of us, and the effect on the water crystals. So, if that is what it will do to water, what is the effect on us as humans? The average adult human body is 50–65% water. If almost 60% of your body is made up of water and it responds to negative thoughts and words uttered by you and those around you, imagine the effect on your body composition and consequently your health? Now there's a thought – mind boggling, I know.

Listen to the words you are telling it – it is a full-time nosey neighbour, always listening over the wall. Your mind has no choice but to respond as it thinks it is in your best interest and what you want. If you want to change something, you must change your dialogue. No excuses now for the way you talk to yourself, because even if no one can hear you speak like you do, you can hear you and that's all that matters. You might not have felt heard as a child but you are heard, your mind never tunes out, it is always listening to the good, the bad and the ugly. Fill your mind with positive words, mantras and statements.

PRINCIPLE # 3
<u>YOUR MIND IS A CREATURE OF HABIT</u>

Your mind loves what it knows and rejects what it doesn't know. Children love to watch the same television programme over and over or read the same story book each night – humans do this because familiarity represents safety and security. This is an early programming dating back to the first evolved human brains that on day one would venture out of the tribe to hunt for food to eat, they might have encountered a ferocious lion near the river on their trip but managed to navigate back to home safety. The next day, they took a similar path but avoided the river as they knew that they would be safe if they didn't go near the lions. They continued to do this knowing that if they stayed close to the route that was familiar, they would be safe. This links back to the first tool I gave to you, the mind's number one role is to keep you alive at all costs, staying familiar keeps you safe. This also applies to relationships, friendships, food, choices, life – you gravitate to things that are familiar even though, at times, they might not be healthy choices. For example, people who grew up with an abusive or absent father often attract a similar kind of partner as an adult because this is what is familiar. I chose boyfriends (up until I met my husband) who were uninterested in me – these boyfriends evoked feelings of not enough and not lovable (my old childhood beliefs), much like I felt with my 'uninterested' Dad. I was attracting the same type of men as my Dad without even knowing it. I was looking for men who elicited the same feelings Dad did because this was familiar. Another thing that was familiar to me was drama – I was addicted to it, yep, believe it or not! I had an energy healer do some numerology and she asked me if I was addicted to anything. I was quite surprised by the question as I wasn't familiar with any addictions but she was adamant there was a deep-set addiction in me – 'ah she said, you were addicted to drama. This came from your childhood and you continued this through to adulthood.' Once she highlighted that to me, I realised she was right and I would attract and create dramatic events because it's what I knew and what was familiar. Despite my conscious longing for a peaceful, harmonious and calm life, my subconscious mind only knew a chaotic household.

PRINCIPLE #4
YOUR MIND IS THE MASTER OF DOMINOES (NOT THE PIZZA KIND)

Every thought created triggers a chain reaction in your body, just like Diana Ross once sang 'I'm in the middle of a chain reaction da da'. Every thought or idea you create cues a chemical release in your body and leads to a physical response. This can be either positive or negative depending on the type of thought or idea created. When you have a thought, it releases a chemical in your body in the form of a hormone. Your thoughts affect all of the functions of your body. Thoughts of worry trigger changes in your stomach, like that butterfly sensation induced by nerves or anxiety. When you feel nervous about something, this constant trigger in the stomach can, in time, lead to ulcers or a similar stomach ailment. Angry thoughts stimulate your adrenal glands and the increased adrenaline in the blood stream causes a variety of body changes. Anxiety and fear attached to thoughts raise your pulse rate and cause a tight feeling in the chest and sweaty hands. Ideas that have a strong emotional content affect us strongly. Once accepted, these ideas continue to produce the same reaction over and over again. Be mindful of what thoughts or ideas you plant because, eventually, they affect your body. It helps to use language that is neutral such as 'this is a challenge' as opposed to 'this is a living hell, it's killing me'.

PRINCIPLE # 5
EXPECTATION IS REAL

When your mind expects a particular outcome, it tends to be created. Many people suffer from chronic anxiety, which is a subconscious mental expectancy that something terrible will happen. You know those people who see everything as glass half empty and always picture the worst possible scenario. Other people seem to be lucky or have a magic touch. Life seems to shower them with blessings for no apparent reason, and so we call them 'lucky'. What seems to be luck is, in reality, positive mental expectancy, a strong belief that they deserve to be successful. 'You are what you think.'

Your physical health is largely dependent upon your mental expectancy. Physicians recognise that if a patient expects to be sick, in pain, paralysed, helpless or even to die, the expected condition tends to be realised. What are you expecting? Disaster? A series of nightmares? Notice your dialogue: maybe you are, without realising, thinking thoughts like, 'I won't get the next job, I just know it' or maybe you're pre-empting conflict in your marriage or that it might fail, or that your partner might leave you. Be careful where you place your energy and what energy you give your thoughts as you will end up creating a self-fulfilling prophecy and you don't want that.

It's true that if you believe something that creates an emotionally induced symptom in your body, such as fear or joy, it will eventually create an effect in the body, in the form of disease or improved health. This is known as the placebo effect. Someone suffering from ill health and disease often has repeated episodes of the symptoms of that disease for some time before organic change can be found. A person who is often fearful will have a nervous stomach that eventually develops ulcers. Tension headaches, irritable bowels, weak bladders, inflexible joints, angry rashes – all can, over time, lead to organic disease. Chronic fear of ill health and repeated suggestion of ill health such as feeling *'pissed off'*, like you *'can't stand it anymore'*, or perhaps you have *'no back bone'* for life, with *'little support'* will in time create the condition. Positive thoughts and positive emotions create positive organic change. The body and mind takes things literally so when you use language such as 'life is killing me' and 'I can't stand this', 'I don't want to hear this any longer', you can unintentionally invite a slow death or a bad leg or a hearing condition. If you convince yourself you are old, your body will respond and start to show signs of an old body to match your core beliefs about old people. That's why nowadays if someone asks my age I say I'm '40 years young!' as opposed to 40 years old!

PRINCIPLE #6
F*CK LOGIC!

Imagination and emotions always defy logic. The only way to challenge an emotion is to challenge it with an alternative emotion – meet fear with excitement. Imagine walking on a tightrope or small plank of wood just a few inches off the floor. Easy, right? Of course, your mind is saying 'yeah yeah babes, I got this, simple, no hassle'. Now move the plank of wood 20 metres off the ground and your inner talk will be very different. 'Noooo, I can't, I might fall, break my leg, hit my head, wobble off. No no no.' Why? Because as soon as you put the images of you falling over the edge into your mind, it will respond to exactly that. Reason is easily overruled by imagination. You must calm that overactive imagination down as it can be debilitating. What the imagination locks on to, the emotions and the body will follow. Imagination accompanied by a strong emotion such as anger, hatred, guilt, or fear, usually cannot be changed simply through the use of reason or talking yourself out of it, you need to go deeper than this. Keep visualising the intended outcome and stay clear of what you don't want and focus only on what you want the outcome to be.

PRINCIPLE # 7
<u>BLUE SKY THINKING</u>

Every proposed idea or suggestion (positive or negative) that is acted upon by you, lowers the resistance to further ideas. The more you are open to ideas, the more you accept them.

When I talk about suggestion, I mean an idea or plan that is put forward for consideration. Once a suggestion has been accepted by the subconscious mind, it becomes easier for other similar suggestions to be accepted and acted upon. This is why in a session I start with simple suggestions to my clients that are unlikely to be refused such as suggesting pleasant sensations for relaxing the body: 'you are drifting gently, calmly, into a relaxed state'. Once these are accepted, subsequent suggestions that are not blocked by a fixed conscious or subconscious idea become easier to follow. By the time I am suggesting to my client that they are enough (a suggestion that, at first, they might have rejected as it was too early to accept it) and that their confidence is radiating from them, they are so far into the session and have been accepting suggestion after suggestion that their mind now accepts them.

If you want to change the way you think, start gently and keep replacing new ideas with bigger ideas and before you know it you will have brainwashed yourself in taking over the world.

PRINCIPLE #8
F@CK WILLPOWER!

Willpower doesn't work because the harder your conscious mind has to work, the less your subconscious will respond. You know that moment when you can't think of the word off the top of your head, it simply will not and cannot come to mind but as soon as you stop thinking about it, the word or name pops in to your...oh what's the word?! Ugh. What is it?! Anyway, you know what I meant. Moving on. Letting go of conscious effort allows the subconscious to act automatically. When the subconscious has a learnt behaviour, this behaviour happens automatically unless it is being repressed by conscious effort or willpower. However, once the conscious effort that is repressing the automatic response is relaxed – which inevitably occurs when the conscious focus shifts to other areas of concern – we move on; the automatic response, behaviour, or condition returns, the word is recalled. Head. That was the word I was looking for.

PRINCIPLE # 9
KEEP BELIEVING

Once an idea has been accepted by your subconscious mind, it remains there until it is replaced by a new idea. These are your habits, the more you do it, the more it becomes a habit. If you decide that you don't want the habit anymore, you have to consistently practise a new habit until that becomes the familiar action and replaces the old one. Once an idea has been subconsciously accepted, it becomes a fixed habit of thinking. The more this thinking is acted upon, the more it becomes a fixed habit of acting. People have habits of thinking as well as habits of action, but the thought or idea always comes first. To change behaviour, it is necessary to change the thoughts and ideas that create the behaviour. So darling, keep growing, opening your mind, challenging beliefs because they are there to be challenged and ultimately changed and upgraded. If we don't? The old beliefs will stay there, you will stay where you are, just like Grandpa who stays stuck in his old ways.

PRINCIPLE # 10
I LOVE YOU BUT I HATE YOU

Your mind cannot hold opposing feelings or beliefs. You cannot be depressed and happy. You can't be tired and wide awake. You can't be confident and anxious at the same or be miserable and elated because it's impossible for the mind to hold such conflicting beliefs and it sends the mind into a frenzy. So a word of advice, when you are at a dinner party, joking about being a failure or not enough, you can't then consciously believe you will succeed while telling failure jokes; your mind doesn't differentiate between a joke or a truthful statement and it locks on to the most believable and easily acceptable belief.

PRINCIPLE #11
YOU CREATE YOU

You are a manifestation of your thoughts and beliefs. As you developed as a child, you picked up beliefs; some served you, others were less desirable, but you took the beliefs as truth and went out into the world to validate them and confirm them. If you look for miracles you will find them, if you look for sadness, anger and despair you will find those too. Be careful what you go out to the world to look for because whatever you are looking for, you will find and eventually you will become exactly that because you believe you have found the evidence and it's been validated. It's just like when you are looking to buy a new car: as soon as you put your mind to it, you can't stop seeing that model or colour of car. Look and you will find. Be mindful of your beliefs, your internal talk, the images in your head. Create a you that you want. You're in charge. You hold the key.

LANGUAGE – THE POWER OF IT

It is so important to pick your words cautiously; as you have learnt, your mind responds to the words you give it. Negative words create negative outcomes (however they manifest), positive words create positive outcomes. I remember when I first trained as a hypnotherapist I went for an interview at a women's clinic to assist women to return to maximum health. I sat at the bus stop terrified, my heart was pumping, my hands were sweating and I was short of breath. I noticed the words I was using as I sat waiting, 'I'm scared, I can't do this, what if I fluff my interview'. As soon as I changed the way I was talking to myself to 'I'm excited, I'm choosing this, I want this', the feelings subsided and my mind began to believe that I was genuinely excited and choosing to embrace this interview.

We all face tricky situations at work or at home, I know I do, particularly when I'm looking after my two children. It's a common turn of phrase these days to say 'this is a nightmare', but it isn't really, is it? It's a challenge, it's an unpleasant struggle but it's not a nightmare and it will pass so how about when you face struggles like this, do you change the way you talk to yourself? 'This is a challenge. I can do this. I am strong.' Your body and mind will respond, your heart rate will lower and you will sail through far better than when you are hyped up saying 'this is a nightmare'.

These simple tools make a huge difference. Remember, I am a product of the process. I have done all of these things to transform my life. It might seem like a lot to take on at first but remember, you are like an onion and you are slowly and gently peeling away the layers to eventually reveal your core, your essence. Keep your focus.

KEY WORDS

Here are some key words that will help you talk to others with more clarity, understand what someone else really means when they are talking to you, and dialogue with your mind even better.

KEYWORD – BUT

Imagine you are with a friend and they say to you, *'I really appreciate you as a friend, I'm glad we see each other every Friday...BUT....'*

Or

'That's a lovely haircut... BUT...'

'You did a great job with this... BUT...'

Everything that the friend has just said before the BUT has been completely ignored and you only listen to the second part of the sentence and you focus on what comes after it – because what comes after a 'but' is really what the person means. The word BUT negates or cancels everything that goes before it. And is generally accepted as a signal that the really important part of the sentence is coming up.

When you use it, most people listening to you will give more attention and more weight to what you say after you say BUT. This tiny little word is widely misused. Another word that is used in the same way is 'however'.

The key to using BUT to maximum effect is when you want to acknowledge something negative but emphasise the positive alternative such as, *'That wasn't your greatest effort BUT I know you will focus more next time.'* The recipient is going to receive this message in a far better way with the negative before the BUT. Bring an awareness to this, notice it when you use it or when others use it in their sentences and you will get a big insight into what they really mean and feel.

KEYWORD – SHOULD

You know when you are talking about something you 'should' do such as: *'I really SHOULD do some exercise tomorrow.'* Or *'I really SHOULD stop eating biscuits.'*

When you insert the world SHOULD it undermines your ability to do something and lessens your commitment to the goal. It also indicates someone else's values, not your own. *'I SHOULD go and exercise because my mother always told me I must'* – this is the mother's value, not yours.

'I SHOULDN'T use a microwave because a television programme told me they are dangerous' – This is the media's values not your own (my own value, however, is that microwaves are toxic. Side note: Get rid of it.)

Notice where you are using the world SHOULD and you will find there is a resistance to whatever it is you are saying you SHOULD be doing. If it is something you would genuinely like to achieve, change the way you are talking with your mind and change the SHOULD to 'I will' and notice the difference it makes to the emphasis and commitment you are making to the task.

KEYWORD – TRY

'Trying is lying', as Marisa Peer would say. When you use the word TRY, it lacks any impetus to do something. When you use the word TRY, you use it when you expect or assume failure.

'We must TRY and meet up soon' actually means something like *'I would rather not see you again and I will pretend that I will, to avoid an awkward situation'*.

'I'll TRY and get that done' means *'I'm not going to tell you I cannot or will not do it – but don't hold your breath!'*

I hear this a lot with people making empty promises, they aren't brave enough to be honest and say, 'I won't get this done' so they think by saying they will TRY, it will lessen the disappointment and avoid any awkward stand-off.

Listen out for this and when someone uses this word or you hear yourself saying it; sound the alarm bells because THEY/YOU DO NOT MEAN WHAT THEY ARE SAYING! Be mindful when you use it, I always recommend being honest and open as long as you talk from a loving and compassionate perspective.

KEYWORD – MY

Be careful where you are using the word MY. Why? When we use the word MY we are claiming ownership of the word it precedes. In many ways this is ok and has no repercussions and its use is fairly innocuous:

'I love MY dog'

'I love wearing MY comfy bed socks at night'

'I like to drink MY tea with milk'.

However, when we use MY before an illness or something negative you may be struggling with, you are claiming this something is yours.

'I can't drink milk due to MY stomach problems'

'I haven't been on holiday this year due to MY cancer'

'I am feeling rather tired today, it must be MY anxiety.'

I'm pretty sure you do not want to own any of these! You want to stay healthy and full of life don't you? Next time you notice yourself using MY next to something you don't want to be suffering with, refer to it in a neutral sense – THE cancer, THE anxiety and only use MY when you truly want to align yourself with it. Got it?

KEYWORDS – I AM

Introducing the most powerful two words you can use. Why? Because when you begin a sentence with I AM you are making a statement about yourself. Whatever follows 'I am' starts the creation of it. Yes, it's true – 'I am' is a 100% pure statement of creation. What statements are you making about yourself? Are they positive or negative? Notice how you are dialoguing with your mind and what you are claiming is yours. As Joel Osteen said, 'What follows the "I am" will always come looking for you. Many times, you are using the power of "I am" against yourself.' What are you looking to create in your life? You get a free preview of that creation by discovering your current 'I am' beliefs.

While you are just learning about the concept of 'I AM' there are bound to be some negative I AMs that you need to change, for example:

☆ I AM STUPID – change to I AM CLEVER

☆ I AM UNLOVABLE – change to I AM LOVED

☆ I CAN'T – change to I CAN

☆ I AM TOO OLD – change to I AM YOUNG

☆ I AM NOT GOOD ENOUGH – change to I AM ENOUGH

☆ I AM LAZY – change to I AM RESPONSIBLE

☆ I AM FAT – change to I AM FIT

☆ I AM ALWAYS LATE – change to I AM ALWAYS ON TIME.

If I AM are creator words, be certain that you are only applying the words I AM to things you want to be or become.

AFFIRMATIONS

Since we are on the subject of language, I'm sure you have heard about using affirmations or mantras but have you ever wondered why they work?

An affirmation is a statement that you say out loud, or to yourself, that affirms what you are or think. When you say something, and repeat it to yourself, it will influence your thoughts. This is why affirmations are so successful. If you say to yourself, 'Today is a great day', you will automatically begin thinking about your day in a positive way. The key with affirmations is they must be in the positive in order for them to assist in the experience you want to have.

Remember: what you focus on, you attract, so begin using affirmations to focus on what you want. Always keep affirmations short so that you can easily remember them and repeat them to yourself multiple times. Your mind may not believe what you are telling it at first but you have to trick it. Your mind learns through repetition, keep saying it over and over and eventually your mind will take on this positive suggestion.

Here are some affirmations I would recommend using to transform your self-esteem:

☆ *I am enough* (my go-to phrase)

☆ *I am lovable*

☆ *I matter*

☆ *I deserve to be happy and successful*

☆ *I deserve a good life*

☆ *I am competent, clever and able*

☆ *I have brilliant coping skills* (I use this a lot in challenging times)

☆ *I love me*

☆ *I am proud to be me.*

VISUALISATIONS

I have shared with you how to connect and dialogue with your inner child and essentially this is a visualisation. You may or may not be familiar with visualisations or why they work but they have been an incredible and ongoing tool for my emotional and physical well-being. First, what is a visualisation? A visualisation is like a mini movie that you create in your head based on a desired outcome. For example, if you wanted to learn how to skateboard, the more you focus your mind on the steps you need to take in order to achieve this goal such as looking forwards, balance, strong legs and focused mind, and the more you imagine you doing this in your head, the quicker your body will respond. Why? Well, it's relatively simple: the mind does not know the difference between real or imaginary. This is the same when you are watching television; when you see something shocking or sad on TV, the way that your mind and body responds emotionally and physically are the same as if you were witnessing the same scene in real life. Your mind cannot differentiate the two; for the mind, the two are the same. When you visualise something, you are technically tricking the mind. Athletes use this tool a lot to improve their technique and to broaden their capabilities. Just like when Roger Bannister achieved the sub 4-minute mile in 1954. Prior to this no man had ever been able to run this fast despite many attempts. As soon as Roger achieved this, more and more people were able to do it. By simply witnessing this new time and knowing that the human body was capable of running at this pace, others were able to imagine it and achieve it too.

I use visualisations a lot to rewrite old scenes and rescue my inner self. When I do this, although it doesn't actually happen in real life as such, it allows the mind to accept that it has, and reframes the old scene so when the mind returns to that scene, it sees it differently and therefore the chemical response to the scene changes.

I also use a visualisation to achieve a desired outcome before an event that I might be fearful of, such as a tricky family situation or big work presentation. I imagine the scene coming up in the way that I want it to unfold. You can do the same. Get really detailed: imagine what the future scenario looks like, smell likes, imagine all the small details, what the other people are wearing – you really want to activate all the senses and the more detail the better. It's like you are putting your mind through a rehearsal and it knows what to expect. Remember, what your mind expects to take place is generally what unfolds.

GUIDED MEDITATIONS

This leads me on to guided meditations and why this tool is also so effective. Much like visualisations, guided meditations work in the same way in that they take your mind through a journey that it can't tell if it is real or not.

What is the difference between meditation and guided meditation? Meditation takes place in your mind and is guided by your own mind. Often when people try to meditate they say things like 'I can't shut my mind off, the mind chatter is so busy' – don't worry that your mind wanders off, just bring it back to the breath. The more you do it, the easier it becomes – remember, your mind learns through repetition. A guided meditation is something you listen to and is guided by someone else's voice, by a narrator. If you find meditating difficult then this is the perfect tool as it focuses your mind on one thing. Make sure you pick one that focuses on what you want to achieve such as a sense of calm, anger release or inner child connection.

Find a method that works for you and do it consistently until the results and goals are met. So often people do something for a few days and drop it. Remember, you are changing a lifetime of old beliefs and a couple of days of meditating or hypnosis aren't going to make those old beliefs vanish. It takes commitment, perseverance and repetition. If you want to change your life, the commitment is only as great as the desire to change. Ensure both are met with big energy behind them, and voila!

You have quite a set of tools under your belt now. There is nowhere to hide, you've had the lowdown on how your mind works – gone are the days when you could blame your complex mind for holding you back and stopping you from being your best self. Say goodbye to procrastination, *you* are in charge, not your mind.

What have I discovered?

What do I want to change?

What do I want to create?

'Shine your *light*

brighter than it's ever

shone before.'

Why Change Matters

chapter six

Darling,

Remember how we used to play? Gosh, how we laughed!

Rolling in the grass with the sunshine on your face. Carefree living, wasn't it?

Let's activate that joy, the love, the magic. It's still inside you somewhere.

It's the simple things in life that bring you the greatest joy – remember that.

Always.

Shine on, Sister!

Love

Your Self-Esteem

'She is clothed in strength and dignity just shining without fear of her power or the future.'

An anonymous quote reinterpreted by Me.

Commitment to change is vital if you want to transform your life. You are now a pro at understanding how to take control of your mind and make it work for you rather than against you. You've now got an understanding of why these mind tools work and how you can use them to your benefit. Explore the various methods and find what works for you. As well as doing this, you must consciously change the world externally, it's not just an inside job but the work starts there.

Your old story – your 'old' story now – is something you were and it was a way of life you used to live. It is no longer you and cannot be a part of you again. That was a former version of you, just like the part of me is 'Old Cat'. You have now chosen a new path and are fully focused, devoted and committed to this new way of life. You see the benefits of making this choice, you can picture the future you, bathing in your future life while blissfully enjoying you in the present moment.

As you stand at the Y-junction of your life, you can see in the left-hand branch exactly what life would be like if you continued making the same old choices, ran the same old patterns, behaved the same, spoke to yourself with the same old negative self-talk, and held on to all the self-limiting beliefs. Does it look good? How does it feel? How are you growing? Old? Or are you blossoming? Are your childhood dreams being fulfilled? Are you swinging from the chandeliers? No? Didn't think so.

How about the right-hand branch? What does life look like there? As you look down this path, life is exciting, you're doing things that are new and thrilling, you're growing, blooming and blossoming. You're free from the old burdens and open to the new adventures that await. Your soul is alight, happiness is here, you have tools to navigate the waves of life, you can feel your infinite magic and capabilities. You are living.

Which path do you choose? The right one, as in the right-hand branch, or the wrong one? Darling, there is no wrong or right, there is life, and life is choice and you have free will. You are the master of your destiny, left or right, right or wrong, lit up or put out, shining or dulled down – it's all a choice.

It was Marisa Peer who introduced me to the concept of our minds liking what is familiar because it makes us feel safe and avoids anything that is unfamiliar. If you match the choice that I made (the right-hand branch) you will be letting go of what has been familiar for a long time but that's all it is. As we now know, the mind likes what is familiar but in order to move forward, you must make the familiar unfamiliar and the unfamiliar[13] familiar. Trust the process; a habit is easily changed when commitment and consistency is applied. Keep your eye on the prize, remember why you are doing this and focus your mind. You are choosing this new life – a life of purpose and fulfilment – you know with every cell of your body why you are doing this.

There may be moments when you wobble, when the ground feels like it is shaking and you want to return to land that is familiar and safe. The old land is barren and the flowers are dying, the grass has dried up and the pond is parched. As the old life falls away you must go to a place of trust, trust that something great is on its way to you. Let go – no holding on, resistance is far more painful and damaging than the letting go. Once you let go, trust me, it's liberating and feels so good. So, know that things will change but always for the better and life will be far greater than it was before. Trust the process.

So what can you expect to change when you embark on this new life?

YOUR TRIBE

When you make the commitment to yourself to upgrade your life, change comes in many different forms, not just letting go of outdated beliefs and transforming your confidence. I

---

13   Copyright Marisa Peer

remember one of my first sessions with my coach and she said to me that many of my existing relationships would not stand the test of time as they were based on my old self. It's the Law of Attraction after all: you attract what you put out there so your friends match that same vibe. This means that when you raise your vibration, you attract a different vibe and tribe.

Now this might seem daunting at first but trust me, either new relationships form or the existing ones become more real and authentic. It's about surrounding yourself with people who make your heart sing, soul smile and eyes light up, and if they don't, then it's time to let go. Remember who you are choosing to become and keep her in your sights. You have made a commitment to her and to yourself to upgrade and change your life.

Start to bring an awareness to this and notice how your relationships make you feel. Ask yourself if you are playing your old role which goes against your authentic self. Whoever is in your life, remember they are there to teach you something; even if that 'something' might not feel good at the time, it is a gift. Often, those who don't make you feel good are there to mirror back what you need to heal in yourself.

Let's explore this a little further, shall we? When a situation, experience, partner, friend, parent or sibling annoys or hurts you, what is actually happening is they are 'triggering' you back to an old memory that you experienced as a child or even in a past life. What happens is we often blame someone else for being 'unsupportive', 'distant' or whatever the feeling might be that has been activated, but this is merely just you projecting your past feelings on a present situation. This was something I had to work very hard to heal and can be a tricky concept to grasp, but trust me, it's 90% the old memory being triggered and 10% the situation or person behaving out of your value system. So before you go mouthing off about that someone p*ssing you off royally, explore what feeling that situation is bringing up and track back to where in your childhood you felt this. Go back to the list of the beliefs from earlier in the book and notice what belief is coming up for you. Not heard? Not valued? Unsupported?

Then there are those people who you have recognised the trigger from, you've done 'the work' (talking to your inner child) and still that person doesn't make you feel good, they're zapping your energy and time, and it's clear they are no longer serving your highest self; then it's time to let go. Don't worry, you don't have to write them off suddenly and completely out of your life, but create a healthy distance and continue to go about your life allowing the distance to grow naturally.

This can feel a little bit like part of you is dying and indeed it is, part of your old self is dying away to make room for your new self. Keep in mind your intention, to shine bright and to be your authentic self. Trust that all of these changes are in your best interest and are meant to be. Remind your inner child that she is loved and it's time for her to let go so that she can truly shine and be herself and that means with people who accept her how she is.

What friends are bringing drama in to your life or gossiping and judging you and others? Where do your friends need you to be broken so that they can swoop in and be the hero? This was a very common theme for me. Many of the relationships that I had formed were based on me being powerless so that I would turn to others for help and support, which would in turn make them feel good about rescuing me. This was all well and good and it was from the best intention from the others, but it taught me that I couldn't take care of myself and needed others to rescue me. I had to re-educate myself and my inner child that we are strong and have all the tools we need to be a success and achieve the goals that we are setting. This is where you need to do the work too. Remind yourself you can cope, you can do it and you no longer need to play a helpless role.

There may be times when others will tell you that you've changed. Always respond to this with a 'thank you' – let's face it, you've worked hard to make the change. At the time this can feel hurtful, like they aren't accepting you. The truth is, the change in you is simply bringing up their stuff and highlighting feelings in them that they don't want to acknowledge so it's easier for them to project onto you and your life. It isn't you, this is their stuff. Stand strong, don't fall back to your old role of people pleasing, you deserve to live the life you are choosing. Remember, you are born to shine and in order to do so, life changes have to be made and this means letting go of everything that no longer serves your highest good.

There were moments of loneliness when I healed this part of me but I wouldn't change it for the world. I am happier than I could ever be. Yes, I have fewer friends around me but I have chosen this path and I now surround myself with people who accept me for my authentic self. Of those friendships that died away, some may come around again and this is just a phase of transition for all involved. I still love those people who have played an important role in my life and the door is always open to reconnect with them, and when that happens it's on new terms with a slightly different Cat, one who is authentic and living her truth and is wholeheartedly happier. The loneliness it brought up was another part of me to be healed and re-paired. It was that little girl in me that felt lonely way back then. I allowed the feelings to come forward for healing, dialogued with my inner child and functionally reminded myself that I have everything I need within and that no one and no 'thing' can make me feel lonely, because as long as I am connected with my soul and inner child, I can never be lonely. Enjoying your own company and time alone is self-love, it is you acknowledging how you love to spend time with yourself and that there is no better company than yourself. How gorgeous is that? You create your own fun, on your own and love it. If you are somebody who struggles with spending time alone then take note, there is work to be done here. What old scenario does it take you back to? What feeling don't you want to feel and instead fill your time with others to stop that old feeling surfacing? Do the work and this will pass and you will grow beyond all measure, I promise.

ATTRACTING YOUR NEW TRIBE

As the layers peel away and relationships that no longer serve you become more distant, it's time to start manifesting your new tribe – those who match your new vibration, support and celebrate your growth. Where do you begin though? Start by noticing what lights you, what new hobbies will you embark on, is there something that you have always wanted to try? Now is the time, don't wait, sweet one, whatever it is that gets the energy buzzing in your body and butterfly excitement in your stomach, that's what you must be doing.

A great thing to do, and something I guide my clients towards, is go back and think about what you loved doing as a kid and take it up again. As you do this you will meet new people who have the same interests as you. My other biggest tip is, trust that the right person or people will arrive at the right time. Set your intention to grow your tribe and attract people with similar values and interests to you and, mark my words, out of nowhere these people arrive. It's not about quantity but quality and you'll begin to notice that although there aren't a bunch of friends surrounding you, those that are there will bring you so much joy because they will be aligned with your new values and accept you as you – the real you.

It's so important to recognise what you love doing, especially in this fast-paced life; you often have no idea what lights you up and even if you do, you allocate very little time to it. It's believed that your passion between the ages of 7 and 14 years old is your life purpose and your gift. Rewind the clock and think back to what you loved doing then. Enough of this constant 9am to 5pm rat-race job and mind-numbing routine, this is about upgrading and activating parts of you that have lain dormant so that you can lead your fullest and happiest life. Of course, not all of us can just change the rat-race job at the click of a finger but we can fill the rest of our time with soul-nourishing activities while we make our grand plans to change careers. Life is a choice and the choices lie in your hands.

Apart from making you excited about getting out of bed each morning, there are so many benefits from living your purpose. Did you know that people who have meaning and purpose in their life have a lower risk of Alzheimer's disease and cognitive impairment in later life. Not just that, but purpose in life is linked to many positive health benefits including:

☆ Better mental health

☆ Reduced depression

☆ Happiness

☆ Satisfaction

☆ Personal growth, self-acceptance

☆ Better sleep

☆ Longer life expectancy

I'd say it's a no brainer, wouldn't you?

Once you find your purpose, your focus changes, that 9 to 5 lifestyle becomes less appealing and the drive for material things and a money-driven life becomes less important. For me, joy now comes from the simplest things, watching a sunset, being by the sea, walking in nature, even trekking with llamas (a recent escapade of mine!). Don't get me wrong, I still enjoy treating myself to a material item but there is little meaning to it now. I don't need things to make me happy if I have joy inside, I honour my creative flow and live my purpose. The money I now make allows me to enjoy more natural fun that expands my mind and nourishes my body and spirit. No 'thing' has the power to do that.

The biggest change for me (which came after just three sessions with my coach once I let go of old pain and hurt) was I couldn't stop reading books. I never read as a kid and used to find picking up a book the most labour-intensive activity; deep inside me, I wanted to be a 'reader' but couldn't muster up the passion or desire to do it. And then BAM! There I was consuming book after book like something in me had been unleashed and activated. Thankfully it meshed very well with my new-found career as I would read book after book about the subconscious mind, the power of the human brain, the Universe and consciousness as a whole and here I am now writing one of my own. You see, it was all just so perfectly aligned and meant to be. Follow your heart, notice what makes your toes twinkle, your eyes light up and your soul sing, that's what you should be doing. I also ended up taking up yoga and ice-skating. Not at the same time, however – yoga on ice could be interesting! You get my gist, as you let go of old stuff, your deepest soul cravings are fed and are no longer starved.

GRATITUDE

Practising gratitude is a very simple tool that changes the chemistry in your mind and body. Tony Robbins describes it perfectly: 'The antidote to fear is gratitude. The antidote to anger is gratitude. You can't feel fear or anger while feeling gratitude at the same time.' This takes us back to Principle 10 – *I love you but I hate you* – your mind cannot hold opposing feelings. Who wants to feel fear? Who wants anger? Not me, I let go of those and one of the best tools for this is to use the emotion of gratitude, because anger (or fear) and gratitude cannot exist within the mind at the same time. Note: this isn't a quick way of avoiding letting go of stored anger (you have a meditation app to do that) but if you are somebody whose go-to resting mood is grumpy or anxious, this is a good remedy to help you move away from that mood and into a place of peace.

So often, one is consumed with what others have, instead of focusing on our internal state and how we truly feel. For example, imagine you're at work and you're really enjoying it, your pay is good, you enjoy the projects that you are working on, you're feeling pretty fulfilled and in a good place career-wise. You then decide to make a cup of tea, and you meet Bob in the kitchen and start chatting. Bob tells you how he is in a good mood today because he just found out he is getting a pay rise, that will be more than you are paid. As you go back to your desk, you sit down and start to think, 'That's not fair, I'm not doing this job for this money that I'm earning, I'm worth more than this, these projects don't pay enough for me to work this hard.' In the space of five minutes you have gone from a place of contentment to a place of resentment all because you have compared yourself with another. What happened to the contentment you felt before? Why does what that other person have matter if you were just satisfied with what you have? If you keep comparing and wanting what another has then you are in for a lifetime of disappointment, you will never have the best car, the most well-paid job, the biggest house, because there will always be someone who has that already. That's not to say you can't manifest all these things but this is about having what you have and not making comparisons with others. If you feel 'less than', then if you look outside of yourself you will find validation for this thought. What you seek, ye shall find and all that. What you focus on, you get. Change your focus, be thankful for what you have. Live in gratitude and you will continue to attract more to be grateful for – it's the Law of Attraction after all.

I practise gratitude first thing in the morning when I wake up and am lying in bed. I say I'm thankful for the peace in my life, my healthy, happy kids, my wonderful husband and my home. I extend this to things that might be taking place that day or the experiences I'm about to have as an advance thank you, in full trust of the day I'm going to have, as if it is done already.

There are lots of ways to practise gratitude – perhaps the last thing before you say goodnight, you might recap your day with gratitude. Find a way to bring it into your life whether it's a time allocated to doing this or just start to be thankful for what you have, not what others have or what you don't have. Change your focus, be present; everything you need, you have within you. What are you grateful for?

MORE CHANGE

What else needs to change as you grow? Well, your world around you will begin to transform as you hatch out of your egg. The solid structure that you had built around you, which once kept you safe, has now reached the point when it is too small to house magnificent you; it's now time for you to break out and crack open for the world to see.

What are you consuming (and I don't just mean food)? What are you filling your mind with in terms of social media, magazines, films, television and books? Do they grow you, do they help you become a better version of yourself? Be honest with yourself. I'm delighted that you are reading this as this implies you're already on to the high vibe kinda thing, so well done. So many women are still unconscious in knowing how the mass media are indoctrinating us to be broken and in need of plastic surgery, fake tan, false eyelashes, hair extensions and so on, to be enough. As you know this is completely untrue. First, those things won't make you feel enough if you are starting out from a place of not feeling enough – there will always be another product that will come with a promise to fix the flaw that you apparently have. Second, you bloody are enough just as you are, you always have been and always will be. My aim in this book is to give you some tough love that will transform your life and make you a better version of you, while giving you hope, real tools and a life to aspire to. Magazines that are constantly talking about how you need plastic surgery to get your man back or go on this diet to make you happy – it's all a load of BS and is so destructive. No one or no 'thing' can make you feel enough; only improving your relationship with yourself will do this. Hollywood movies are so often about a woman chasing the man and without him, she is empty and lost. Untrue. You are your hero, no man will rescue you, only you can rescue you. So be mindful of what you are reading and watching.

YOUR DIGITAL DETOX

I have already touched on social media. A lot is written about it and the problems it is creating in society with it becoming one of the most addictive habits there is. I agree that we all need to learn to use it in a healthy and balanced way, where we can live without it. There is good in social media and, certainly for me, it has given me a place where I can flood my mind with positive affirmations, inspiring lives and places to visit. It has connected me with like-minded people and even given me some new friendships, formed over the digital airwaves. Notice what your social media feed is making you feel – is it a good feeling or not so warm and fuzzy?

WHAT'S EATING YOU?

What do you fuel your body with? Is it with love or hate? Believe it or not, the way you eat matches the way you feel about yourself. Old Cat used to malnourish herself, eat carbs until the cows came home and comfort eat when angry. Now this was all well and good before the so-called midlife spread took hold after having two kids; I got away with it, size 8 was the body I naturally had although my view of my body was always 'it could be better'. The relationship between my weight and myself has been an eye-opening lesson – while I hated myself, the weight was there to protect me from the unkind words I used on myself. The weight was a barrier and protective coating. It has forced me, no matter what size or shape I am, to love me, to love me inside and to accept my outside. I had placed a lot of value on my looks – it was how I got connection, it was the trophy that Dad appreciated, it was the thing that got me boyfriends, it was my credit. But as life went on and retaining a size 8 body after two children became harder, it pushed me to dig deeper and re-pair that part of me that was in need of TLC. I have worked tirelessly on this, to understand the link between my body and my emotions and I can finally say that I am in a place of self-acceptance, often self-love and gratitude for what my body has done for me. When I am in this space I nourish myself, make healthy balanced choices that are in line with greatest version.

Food has its own frequency too. Fast food, processed junk, factory made, chemical laden, Frankenstein food, is all low vibe, it doesn't make you feel good, it has detrimental effects on your mind and body. When you're in a low vibe place, you want low vibe food. Raise your vibration and you raise the roof on your energy levels by fuelling your body with real, wholesome, clean food that enables your body to bloom, blossom and flourish. Notice how you are choosing to feed your mind and body. When we feel inadequate, we have little time or want to care for ourselves and this is with food too. Stop making excuses that you're too busy to eat well. Nuts, fruit and veg don't take long to fuel your body. Remember it's all about choices. Are you choosing to fuel, nourish and nurture your body with food that will activate your life force? Plant food is my favourite form of food because you are literally eating the sun's energy and life force. That's not to say I'm a vegan or a strict vegetarian although I eat few meat products because I care for animals and feel better without meat. Whatever choices you make, go high vibe and make choices that will assist you in being your best self.

As you change, believe it or not your music, fashion and brand choices will face an upgrade too. It's all about filling your mind and body with good, high vibrational choices for everything that is in your life if you are wanting to create a positive and happy life, full of love, joy and peace. The Beach Boys knew what they were doing when they wrote the song, 'Good good good, good vibrations...'. Pop that on, dance around your kitchen and welcome in your new life. You are the master of your life and creating a life you love.

What have I discovered?

What do I want to change?

What do I want to create?

☆

Congratulations

You have completed steps 1 & 2

A celebratory gift awaits!

Bonus Download

Heart Opening Guided Meditation

(Check out the resources in the back of this book)

Unlocking Your Superpowers

step 3 – create
chapter seven

Darling,

Quit the doubt, you can do it, you were born to do it!

The world needs you.

You've got this!

Trust me. Now go and show the world what it's been missing all this time!

Shine on, Sister!

Love

Your Self-Esteem

> *'Be the kind of woman who when your feet hit the floor each morning the world says, "Yes, she's awake! Good things are coming!"'*

An anonymous quote reinterpreted by Me

My heart is bursting with excitement and love, you have made it through Steps 1 and 2 and here you are in all your glory, ready, willing and open-hearted, waiting for the magic to ensue. This is a mega magical moment, you have flowed effortlessly through the book, learning how your old beliefs have held you back, facing stuff you have pushed down, you have ploughed on knowing that by learning the tools and actively making a commitment to changing your life, you can do it and now, right now, you're here, about to embark on the creation that is your life. This is, hands down, the best part because you become the creator of your life – just say the word, manifest the dream and there you have it, your wish will be delivered.

Before we get creating, I have to give you a science lesson so that you understand why your wish is your command. It's this metaphysical stuff that blew my mind and I realised that all the hippy dippy stuff really wasn't hippy dippy at all, it is simply science and for some reason, don't ask me why, who or how, it got a bad rap and got labelled incorrectly. This isn't just for the hippies of the world, tree huggers, shamans, psychics, mediums, magic makers, wizards, witches and goblins! This is for you, the open-minded, full-hearted, wise and wild woman that you are and it will be your most powerful tool as you embark on creating the life that you want and have dreamt of. This stuff should be taught in schools, every child should and must be educated on the laws of the Universe and how everything is available to us if we put our mind and power behind it. Here's why.

THE BIGGER PICTURE

There are a million and two reasons why you matter; let me show you how infinitely magnificent you are because you are more than just a human being living life on planet Earth. Have you ever wondered if there was more to life on planet Earth or if there is such a thing as heaven and who is that man called God? Don't worry, this isn't a religious rant so no need to panic. I have never believed in the concept of God but I do believe there is something greater than us at work. There are many words used to describe this higher power, some call it consciousness, others refer to it as the Universe, Source or Buddha. They are all the same thing but have been given their own names and interpretations. As a kid, I would often lie on my back and look up at the stars and wonder about infinity and the complexities of what is out there but never got answers until I began reading books on quantum physics and metaphysics. You see, it's all science, it's not magic, mystery or about some man with a white beard. Everything is energy and there are universal laws at play which I will go into in detail in a moment. For now, I just want you to know, there is something greater than your reality at play. An infinite power. Still with me? There is such a thing called higher consciousness. This is a spiritual and mystical awareness, it is thinking outside of the 9 to 5 thoughts, getting annoyed about being late or dropping food on your top. It's about seeing the bigger picture when you have an argument with someone. When things happen in my life, I ask myself, what am I being shown here, why do I need to see this, what do I need to heal? Energy speaks and it's talking to us in many ways. This is about seeing yourself as part of something bigger – the Universe. You are a magnificent piece of brilliantly created energy that has been willingly created by something, somewhere, somehow. In raising your awareness beyond your normal thought processes, you can experience your true nature and potential, and I promise you won't believe your eyes. With an awakened higher consciousness you can live in wonder and delight as you create a life you want. Make no judgements, look on with curiosity, as you unlock your potential and let go of your limitations, because you are limitless.

We all work from this one infinite power, every single sentient being and thing on this planet is governed by this power. We can't see it but it's there. Just like we can't see energy or electricity but we know it's there. This infinite power is what everyone and everything is governed by. Although you may not consciously be able to recite the laws to me, your deep, innate, natural, intrinsic programming lives and runs by these. Just like a plant knows how to grow perfectly towards the sun.

I have talked briefly about the Law of Attraction but now we will dive deeper and explore the power that is the Universe and how you can use it to transform your life. The first and fundamental law is that of Attraction which has existed since the dawn of time, whenever that was, and it wasn't something that was just stumbled across one fine day, more like realised. Someone, sometime, way back when, had an abstract thought and put it to the test, culminating in what is now called a law because it cannot be changed or manipulated; it exists and it's real even though we cannot see it.

What is it exactly? Ahh that's the cool bit, simply put by *The Secret*, 'Everything that's coming in to your life you are attracting in to your life. And it's attracted to you by virtue of the images you are holding in your mind. It's what you're thinking. Whatever is going on in your mind you are attracting to you.' #fact. You are like a walking talking magnet (and I don't mean the sexy kind, but that's cool if you're into that), you attract what you put out there with your thoughts and draw it towards you. It starts with a thought and that thought has its very own vibration.

'More!' I hear you shout! OK, here goes. Every thought you have is energy and comes with its very own vibration and frequency so if your mind is putting out a thought like 'I'm lovable', the frequency of that thought, let's say 528Hz (which is the frequency of Love according to Dr Leonard Horowitz), will draw in other thoughts and things in line with that frequency because you attract what you put out and what you put out will come back in the same frequency. This is why it is so important to clear out all the old doo-doo so that you are calling back what you consciously want, not what your deep subconscious programming is, i.e. 'I'm not lovable'. This is why you are the magician, the master, the creator of your life because you can control your thoughts and therefore you can control what you draw in. No more of this victim status, hopeless, helpless shenanigans and there is no excuse now, you are not a victim of how your life is unfolding, you are the master of it, good or bad, right or wrong, it just is and you just are. Philosophers, poets, authors, musicians, scientists, creatives, artists and even billionaires have known this for aeons. This is how life is and this is how you can make life work for you.

Know this too, the Law of Attraction doesn't differentiate between you, a rock star or a dog having a thought or putting out a frequency. There is no hierarchy of who gets what back. It's impersonal and it doesn't filter the good or bad stuff, it simply mirrors back what you are sending out. Life is one big mirror. So sit for a moment and take a look at what has unfolded in your life. What have you been calling in? Because what you have been calling in is a reflection of what you are feeling, thinking and being internally.

Now that we have deleted old programming and changed the way you think, you have a blank canvas to work from and build your life exactly how you want it! Bloody brilliant, this law, isn't it? When it's working for you, that is. It's simple really but so many people are unconscious to a law that is so crucial to the way life is and unless we educate ourselves and the next generation then life will continue to unfold where we feel powerless to our circumstances. Now remember I said at the beginning of this chapter that we are all hooked up to this infinite source and ruled by these same laws, this goes for the thoughts that we are putting out collectively. When groups, countries and our world put out fear-based thoughts and vibrations, we get back that too. With that in mind, look at the state of our planet: isn't this the perfect (not in a good way) reflection of the global consciousness? That's why it starts with you: raise your vibration, it's infectious. Lead by example, be the light, if you don't start the process then who will the others follow? The mass media who scaremonger and fill our minds with fear? No, choose love, choose happiness, choose to orchestrate an internal view that vibrates so high you are bouncing off the walls of life. This stuff is contagious, spread the love, spread happy thoughts, be kind, smile lots because when you do others feel it – it's energy and it is high time you put out high vibe, high end energy to the world because right now the planet needs you and your light, your smiles, your warmth and compassion. When you find these things in yourself, you find them in others. It's your time to shine. Step up, be the teacher this planet needs. Every time you change yourself for the better, another woman changes too, you are an example of what can be done. This is my story, make it yours.

This is why self-love is so important as it is the work you do internally so that you are projecting externally the beautiful vibration of love – let's call it 528! I love that – I'm feeling so 528 today. How about you? So imagine this, if you're putting out a 528 signal, you're gonna get back the same and that might come in the form of friends that love you, a partner, colleagues, friends, family and so on. When you love you, others feel it and you draw in the same love right back at ya. The flip side of the coin is, if you're putting out thoughts and feelings of not lovable or not enough, your reality will reflect this back. You create your reality, you manifest your life.

I can hear some panic ensue as you momentarily have a negative thought. Fear not! First, because negative thoughts are of a low vibration and therefore more dense in energetic terms, they take longer to process and return; so don't worry, there is a delay with the low vibe stuff. The Universe takes the predominant feeling and thoughts that you are emitting, not just one tiny little naughty thought! As Michael Beckwith from the Agape Spiritual Centre says, 'You must be aware, that it has been scientifically proven that an affirmative thought is a hundred times more powerful than a negative thought.' So park the worry (pointless use of energy right there) and move on, let the thought come and go and let go of any attachment to it. Gone, goodbye, cheers.

If you draw in something you cannot understand as you consciously or knowingly didn't put it out there, don't worry, our minds can run on autopilot. Notice what you have drawn in, bring an awareness to the feeling it brings up, locate the emotion and do the work on clearing out this old memory. I often then use hypnosis or a guided meditation because it clears out your subconscious. A good gong bath (a therapeutic sound and vibrational practice designed to heal by clearing energy blocks) or sound bowls can do this too. I love a gong bath. If you don't know what one is, it must sound ridiculous. It's when someone plays the big gong and bathes your body in the vibrations and sounds that are of an incredibly high frequency (that of the Universe, they say) and realigns all your cells, reorganises your subconscious and makes way for magic. If you are feeling good, you will be vibrating at a healthy, happy frequency; if you feel bad, you will be oscillating and drawing in low vibe stuff. Clean up your old programming, understand what you are feeling and readjust your frequency.

Another key point to note down is, thoughts become things. They don't just stay out there in the energetic, unseen world of thought. They manifest into scenes, people and situations, and in doing so, create a tangible representation of your inner dialogue. So does this mean you thought about a yucky event like a car accident and it happened? No, not as such, it doesn't mean that you have to literally have that thought, although that is possible too. It's more that by having those thoughts you were vibrating at that frequency and drew in a scenario that was on the same frequency. So tidy up your frequency and see the evidence unfold. Play with this concept. Upgrade and you will see the results. While I finished this book in Camber Sands by the sea, I was absolutely taken aback at what I had drawn in – sunsets, sunrises, a full moon, a vast beach with soft sand and stunning dunes on my doorstep, the most wonderful boutique hotel, and the list goes on. I was being delivered the most magical reflection of what I felt inside and despite knowing all about this work and the magic of the Universe, it took my breath away. I was on high vibration and wrote from a place on that same frequency. With that said, you will be feeling this high vibe and hopefully will be flying high on the magic carpet with me as you feel my energy as I write.

On that note, you must know that your reality is yours, mine is mine. The way in which your life is perceived by you is based on all your subconscious memories, feelings, scenes, setbacks, laughter and cries – these are very different from mine, as you can imagine. I often use the example of a woman walking down the street when she gets wolf-whistled at. Depending on her past, her beliefs, her feelings she might react with a thought of 'Oh how nice, still got it girl!' and feel happy about it or she might go in to thoughts of fear because she was once attacked by a man who found her attractive.

The point is, the way that you or I might interpret the very same situation is very different because our computer's hard-drive has got different content. Whose reality is right? What is real, what is not? If that lady who felt fear described the situation to her friend it would be a very different story from the one told by the lady who felt happy. What is real? What is your reality based on? Thought provoking, I know, and one to mull over when you have a cross word with someone. Don't always think of how you see things, think of others too. You create your reality and your reality is very different from mine but we are all one. Raise your vibration, attract your reality. I have gifted you a blank canvas and your life and the world is now your oyster. Paint, draw, sketch the life you want, adorn the walls of your reality with your art. You are the artist of your life. Here's your paintbrush.

☆ IN THE SPOTLIGHT ☆
CREATING YOUR LIFE CANVAS

☆ *Write down your new beliefs.*

☆ *Write down how you choose to feel.*

☆ *Write down what you want to draw into your life.*

When you have done that, trust it has been done, know and believe with every cell of your body that you are now drawing this in; time just has to catch up.

It's really important that when we detail what it is we want, we have to think about it like it has already happened.

Trusting with unwavering and unshakeable confidence that it will happen and I promise you, it will. You must act, think and behave like it has already been sorted. Take action every day, trusting that it is all in hand. On a side note, this doesn't mean if you wish to win the lottery you will win – that would require absolute unshakeable belief in the chances of you winning (approximately 1 in 14 million in the UK), having no negative associations with winning the jackpot and not wanting or needing it from a place of lack (which let's face it, a millionaire isn't going to spend the time manifesting the lottery). Remember, hand over to the greater power and laws that are and let it be (as Paul McCartney once sang). The Universe responds in feelings; if you feel it will happen, it will. Feel it to believe it. Let go and don't intellectualise the process, just allow and it will flow. Be open to receiving, open your heart, your mind and your world, and the rest will follow.

NO TIME LIKE NOW

I bet you are wondering how long you have to wait until you receive the manifestations and works of art. That I can't tell you, but hear this, time doesn't actually exist! Yep, you heard it here first. Humans have a tendency (another thing we are taught incorrectly in schools) to go by the clock in everything we do, but as Einstein alludes, there is no such thing as time and everything is happening simultaneously. Rhonda Byrne states in the bible that is *The Secret*, 'If you understand that there is no time, and accept the concept, then you will see that whatever you want in the future already exists. If everything is happening at the one time, then the parallel version of you with what you want already exists'. I told you, this is mind bending, boggling, eye-opening stuff that we should all be educated about as kids. I now talk about these concepts with mine because the bold truth is, it's not woo woo, it's science and it's time we began to share the knowledge as if it's a normal and routine code for life because that is what this is. It's a code for life and you hold the passcode.

PLEASE ENTER YOUR PASSCODE HERE
TO MOVE ON TO THE NEXT CHAPTER –

Magic Moments

— — — —

What have I discovered?

What do I want to change?

What do I want to create?

☆

'Your *light* is here to
illuminate the world.'

Magic Moments

chapter eight

Darling,

Some might doubt your magic but I never have. You are truly magical and so is the Universe that created you.

Together, with unshakeable belief, you, me and the Universe can create a mind-blowing life as soon as you say the word. I'm ready.

Shine on, Sister!

Love

Your Self-Esteem

> *'Let your light shine, it's the greatest gift you can give the world!'*

An anonymous quote reinterpreted by Me.

It's time now to give you the tools to create the life you want and used to dream of as a kid before life got in the way. Well done, you have done a remarkable job thus far; you've finally got some clarity on the stories and limiting beliefs that you had been walking around with and hopefully got to the root of them. Or maybe you are slowly defrosting and warming up to the concepts in this book. Either way, the fact that you are still reading shows your commitment to yourself. Keep chipping away and working on letting go of what no longer serves you. If this book has given you the opportunity to release old emotions and reframe the past then good on you. You have come a long way, pat yourself on the back, let the praise in and congratulate yourself for getting this far. Remember, I said at the start of the book, this process takes courage to even entertain this new way of thinking and change your life, but it's worth it.

Now, it's the fun part and mark my words you are going to have some fun playing with the Universe and its power. You get the gist, this isn't really magic, it's science. Nothing more, nothing less, no tricks. Science. Now, before you baulk at the woo woo, hippy dippy bit, please bear with me. This was foreign to me up until five years ago, although I must admit, I did love visiting a tarot reader when I was a teenager and did always wonder, when I lay under the stars as a kid, was there more to life and death than just black at the end? Once I detoxed my emotions and began to read more science-based books on the mind and its capabilities, the power of the mind-body link, that emotions were simply energy and energy is everything, I realised I was on to something – I was late to the party but that didn't matter. I was hooked. It was Michelle Zelli who said to me in my first session, 'your mind's all furred up, like an old telephone wire (you know those old curly, stretchy ones) and it's time to de-fuzz it'. I didn't know what she was talking about but I went with the flow. When you detox your emotions, you get back in tune with yourself and your intuition becomes a superpower, your gut instinct will guide you. You may be experiencing this already, and if not it's only a matter of time, wondering what those sensations are in your gut and how to manage them. Now that you are able to 'feel' and recognise your emotions, you are in tune with you, your energy and your ability to create a life you want. These superpowers don't exist, or rather, are hidden until you do your mind detox because you have buried your feelings for so long that your subconscious is on another trajectory, seeking out a life aligned with your subconscious programming. As your frequency has gone up, so has your vibration. Let's explore the magic further, shall we?

TRUST

HAND IT OVER

I'm going to ask you to do something that goes against everything you have learnt to date (outside of my book, of course) and ask you to hand over you, your life and the path you are taking to something greater than you. When I am faced with a situation (good or bad) or a challenge, instead of judging it (which we all know is a big 'no-no'), I ask myself, 'what is this challenge showing me, how can I learn from this, where is the gift?' When you undertake the path of healing, transformation, finding yourself or whatever you choose to call it, you gradually peel away the layers and each time you are faced with a challenge that brings up emotions, you are being offered the chance to remedy that unhealed part of you. If you choose not to, and decide to bury or numb that old feeling, it will, without a shadow of doubt, come back and slap you in the face even harder. Try it and see, or rather do it the easy way and trust me on this!

When you can raise your head above the minutiae of life, you take yourself out of the drama and see your life and its lessons as part of a much bigger picture. There is a path, everything is right there waiting for you, you have free will and can choose to take this path this lifetime, or you can avoid healing your wounds and take them through to your next life or lesson. It's down to choice. I choose this lifetime to move forward into another dimension, where I hand over to a much bigger consciousness. I have chosen to develop my conscious awareness of life and how we are all just part of one massive consciousness and energy source. We are one.

When I hand my life over to this theory, it makes each day much easier to navigate as I trust that I have been sent this challenge for a reason and when I do the work (mostly inner child dialogue), I remove another layer and move a step closer to my soul purpose, that dream I had as a kid.

Last year, I was on my way to the airport with my husband and two children and we were running very late for the flight. Before we left, I had also read on the internet (big error) about various strikes at the airport so flights were apparently in chaos. Travelling with or without kids had always been a trigger; it took me back to when I was a child and Mum would be frantically packing up the car, me, two brothers, two dogs, loads of luggage and the kitchen sink and Dad would stroll in, somewhat stressed that it wasn't complete, cue Mum and Dad cross exchange of words. Mum was frustrated that Dad wasn't there to help and Dad was annoyed about Mum not being ready for the big road trip. Anyway, it made for a very fraught and unpleasant start to most family holidays. They are a time when you are supposed to be excited but a massive bucket of cold water had just been thrown over it, enough to quash that sense of excitement and anticipation. Consequently, following those chaotic starts to the holiday, I would replicate Mum's energy when I was packing up for my own family holiday. My husband could not understand why I would get so stressed when I always had it under control but would still manage to turn it into a stressful situation. Once I recognised that this was 'Mum's stuff' and no longer mine, I could talk to my inner child and reassure her that she is safe, and it's okay to be excited about the holiday. The most important thing I had to do though was trust. Trust that we would make the plane, trust that there would be no traffic, trust that everything would be A-ok. And of course, it was – we made the plane with ample time. You see, I was recreating the scene that was familiar to me. I chose to make the familiar unfamiliar and move away from this. That I did. I now go on holiday, despite having packed up the house, two kids and one dog, feeling pretty chilled. Don't get me wrong, I'm not perfect (we aren't meant to be), but I have come a long way from a few years ago.

MANIFESTING

WHAT'S IT ALL ABOUT?

You have heard about this before and I know, just like me, you've done the lottery on a Friday night, talked with your friends about how you will spend the winnings, believed that you WILL win and then come 10pm, you have checked the numbers and you didn't win. WTF? This manifesting malarkey is a load of junk, I believed I would win and I didn't. I give up. Yep, that was me, I even bought myself a bottle of top notch champagne with a lottery ticket in anticipation of my win – I returned it the next day to the supermarket with my tail between my legs. How could I have been so silly to believe that I would win?

Well, I'm here to tell you, this sh*t is real and I now manifest what I put out there and the Universe delivers. Now that's not to say that I can simply manifest a massive lottery win but I might win a tenner! As long as you put out your intention, the Universe will deliver in some way or another. So what is manifesting? It is your creative power and the ability to convert the energy of your thoughts into a newly materialised form. Manifestation is the result. Beginning with one intention at a time, you can learn how to manifest anything in your life. The reason why it doesn't work 'for you' before an emotional detox is because you are still manifesting but you're manifesting things you don't want. These things are aligned with your limiting beliefs, such as not getting that promotion, and were manifested on the back of your subconscious thoughts of 'I'm a failure, I'm so unlucky, nothing goes my way, I'm not enough'. As you can see, you were creating but it wasn't quite what you had in mind until now.

GOALS

WHAT ARE THEY?

I talked earlier about the importance of goals and, that most of the time, we forget to actually set out what we want, let alone think about it. We end up in a place on the sofa where we moan about how life is currently, how we long to be rich and live a life of freedom when we reach 65 years old. But how are we creating how life looks at 65? Or even if we could reach that goal before then? And how would that look? This is really important to get clear so that you know what you are working towards and can take action towards it and therefore achieve it. How can you manifest a life you want when you haven't got clear on what it is you want?

Now you are done with those old feelings of not enoughness and you have cleared out lots of low vibe emotions, leaving you brimming with oodles of confidence, allowing us to get clear what you want. Go back to the goals you set earlier and see if those are still what you want and, if not, redo your goals. Get clear in your mind what you really want out of life. Do you want to change your job, your relationship, where you live, the type of life you are living? How does that life look and feel? If you were to change your relationship, do you mean entirely? And how does this new person look? What traits do you want him to have? Or do you love the relationship you're in but you would like to upgrade it, improve it or return to ways you used to be together? Get it crystal clear. Do you have the level of freedom or money (abundance) that you want or need in order to live a happy life? If you want more freedom or money, how could you manifest a life that brought in abundance? What job would you do? What about smaller goals, such improving your fitness or the way you eat, or integrating more mindfulness into your life?

I'm going to get you to list below three things that you would like to achieve or create. Start small and build from there. For example, I started with: I would like to include more yoga in my life. Well, actually, truth be known, I started with 'I want to get my leg over my head in the first week and practise yoga 6 days a week.' I quickly realised this wasn't realistic and readjusted my goal ensuring it was realistic. I didn't put any timeline on this and just set my intention; I 'put it out there' and ensured that I took action regularly in line with my goal. For me that was managing one yoga session a week, sometimes two (a far cry from my original 6 days a week target!).

A key coaching tool that I use when I'm helping clients reach their goals is ensuring their goals are SMART and in order to make sure goals are clear and reachable, each one should be:

☆ **Specific** – Get really clear on your goal and make sure it is significant enough that you will keep your focus on achieving it.

☆ *Measurable* – Decide how you will be able to recognise that it has been achieved, how you will measure this. What tangible things will confirm that the goal has been reached?

☆ *Achievable* – Be realistic and honest. You often set yourself goals that are too big as a way of sabotaging. If the sight is set too high, there is no hope of achieving it before you have even started.

☆ *Relevant* – Ensure the goals aren't over the top and are reasonable, realistic, rewarding and results-based.

☆ *Time bound* – Put a realistic timeline on this that is achievable and appropriate.

By setting your goals in line with the SMART targets you set up your mind to achieving. Success then becomes a habit and is familiar to you. When you set unrealistic and unattainable goals, your mind gets used to failing, quitting and ends up sabotaging the process to protect yourself from falling flat on your face.

CREATE YOUR VISION

Vision boards are an amazing tool for getting your thoughts out of your head and onto paper (or, these days, on your phone). When we create a vision board we are creating a tool that creates constant, repetitive and focused attention in line with what we want to create. It keeps your consciousness on board and fully engaged with your desires. It all links back to the Law of Attraction and it draws in what we are calling in and putting out there. If we truly believe in what we want and repeatedly create focus, then the Universe cannot fail to deliver. As you visualise what you want, you send out a frequency and the Law of Attraction states that this will be matched. One of the key things for a vision board is that in addition to putting images of what you want, you must include words about how you want to 'feel' because this is the emotion behind the desire. Include images of things that evoke those feelings, or rather, good vibes. Before you know it those feelings and vibes will be coming straight back in your direction. It's the law (of attraction!)

☆ IN THE SPOTLIGHT ☆
CREATE A LIFE YOU WANT

List below five things that you would like to achieve or create.

Rules: Start small. Build from there. Remember, make your goals realistic.

Make sure you are specific and all in line with the SMART targets.

As you achieve these goals, set bigger goals and grow from there.

Now you can move on to setting bigger goals, exploring them and checking they are in line with your strengths, such as moving job or changing partner.

In order to manifest, you need to set your intention, based on your goal. My intention was, 'I will include yoga in my life from today'. Whatever your goal, you must take daily action towards it, whether it is looking up yoga locations, booking the class, clearing out your gym gear and finding the kit; but the rule is you have to move energy in order to show the Universe you're serious and that you mean business. You can't just put out your intention and not do a thing to help create it. Show willingness, show you are serious, keep your focus and the Universe WILL deliver, I promise. As Michelle Zelli says, 'Don't take my word for it, go and play with this concept and get your own evidence.' Still today, I test this notion and before I drive to somewhere busy I say, 'Universe deliver me a parking space, right by the venue.' I then take action with my internal talk, 'I know I will find a perfect parking space, I trust, I believe.' No word of a lie, this works nine out of ten times I do it – it still amazes me and I'm old hat at this now.

Often at night, I set my intention for the next day: 'I will wake up tomorrow focused and ready for my job interview, knowing that I will be just fine.' If you sleep on an intention, when you wake up, your mind picks up from that last thought and remembers it. It's as if you embed it in your subconscious and every cell of your body, so it knows what to do and how to act and feel. It's like a command to your brain – remember your brain responds to the pictures and words you give it.

SETTING INTENTIONS

THE POWER OF THEM

I have touched on the notion of setting intentions and I wanted to explore this a little more with you and show you how and why setting intentions is so important. This is all linked to the way you are dialoguing with yourself and with the Universe. Not only is it important to set small intentions, 'to be kind each day, to be calm ahead of my meeting,' whatever that intention might be, but you also have a bigger intention to fulfil. Like a flower that comes from a seed, when that seed is planted it knows to grow towards sunlight, through the soil, to ultimately bloom. Everything in nature has an intention, from an ant, to a penguin, to a leaf or bumble bee. Each and every one of those things knows at a deep level what its intention is and the job they have to do to in the circle of life. You too have an intention, a life plan, a purpose. It's time to return your focus to that grand plan and relinquish control and trust in the process. It's all about setting an intention with a strong purpose or aim, as well as having unshakeable focus and determination to produce a desired result.

It is no good to just set your intention and leave it at that. Let me reiterate, you must consciously 'hand over' and connect with that greater path, pay attention and trust. I connect with my ultimate intention and purpose on a daily basis. Wayne W. Dyer suggests tools to connect with your intention: 'to establish a relationship with Spirit (aka Source/Consciousness/Universe/God) and access the power of this creating principle is to continuously contemplate yourself as being surrounded by the conditions you wish to produce.' (Side note: Don't be put off by the G-word; I use Universe but, whatever it looks like to you, it is that greater consciousness or energy that connects everything – the stars, moon, us, the planets, everything and beyond). Keep evaluating and noticing if your life as it is, is in line with the future that you are choosing to create. Is it in line with your intention?

CREATIVITY

Your intentions are intrinsically linked to your creativity. When you are weighed down by low vibe emotions, your creativity is the first thing that you lose touch with. This has been an amazing discovery for me; for most of my life, I have struggled with being creative. I mean, I was good at art but it was always a challenge to write, draw, or create something from scratch. I went as far as describing myself as 'not a creative person' – wow, what a statement that was. If I was owning that statement, my mind had to respond and would literally put up mental blocks so I couldn't access my creative brain. Of course, this belief was linked to not feeling enough and it had shut down my creative self and muddied my path to my ultimate intention/purpose. When you are creative you are trusting (that word again!) your own purpose and having an attitude of unwavering intent in your daily thoughts and activities. Staying creative means giving form to your personal intentions. When I let go and trusted my intention, my creativity flowed and continues to do so now. When I'm triggered, it's the first thing that goes and shows me I need to do some work on myself so I can move forward towards my life goal. Meditation is key to keeping your mind clear and your heart free and I cannot emphasise the power of meditation as part of your daily practice.

When I detoxed my emotions, I set an intention to pursue a career in something that lit me up. I never knew I was a healer as such, but I have since had sessions with energy healers and numerologists – I have the life number 1, which is the number of a healer. This came to me after just five sessions with my coach. She had unlocked my passion for reading and I consumed book after book on the subconscious mind, the power of intention and the Universe. There was something afoot, why was I so fixed on this subject? A couple of months later, out of the blue I received an email from Marisa Peer about the hypnotherapy school that she was setting up. I had never signed up for anything of hers and was perplexed and overwhelmed by the synchronicity of this email. The only thing I had seen of her work was a YouTube video with her talking about the biggest epidemic affecting humanity, feelings of 'not enough'. I knew I liked her work. I spoke with her immediately and that night I paid the deposit and was on my path to become a trained hypnotherapist. It felt so right, in my gut, there was no question. As I reflect on my past and see how it has set me up for today, I am convinced without a shadow of a doubt that my challenges have formed me. Without my past, there would be no Cat Raincock coach and hypnotherapist and let alone author, and there would certainly be no book, as I wouldn't be able to guide you and your low self-esteem back to full strength, if I hadn't walked the walk myself.

SYNCHRONICITIES

TRUE MAGIC AT PLAY

This leads me on to that beautiful and magical word, synchronicities. Have you bumped into an old friend you'd been thinking about, heard a song that links so perfectly to the thought you were just having, or maybe you were talking about elephants and you suddenly see a billboard with an elephant on it. Coincidence? Or just a random moment that isn't worth another thought? Do you hear yourself say, 'what a coincidence?' as you marvel at the timing of the coincidence occurring? Well, you shouldn't, because every single coincidence brings a message to you. In fact, there are no coincidences and accidents — there's only synchronicity, and everything happens for a reason. The truth is, everything in life is linked. From the past, to the present and future — every single coincidence or accident you stumble upon is linked. No matter how small or big, it is all about synchronicity. Whether you feel like you are having a great day and everything is going as planned, or having a bad time and encountering a series of 'bad luck' – well, my friend, the Universe is sending you a message. People and things happening at exactly the same moment is nothing but synchronicity. When you trust this concept, and bring an awareness to this, you will start to notice the magic. When synchronicity occurs, explore the message; usually it is showing you are in alignment with your purpose, or it's giving you some advice, maybe by way of song words or a magazine article title towards your purpose. There is a message; listen closely, stay alert. The Universe is on your side, it wants you to succeed.

This book came about because I read and noticed the messages being sent to me. First via a tarot card, which took me aback at first: 'Write? Me? Pah ha ha! Weird'. I kept the card and put it by my bed. The more I looked at it, the more I thought, 'Yeah maybe I could. I always wanted to share my message and perhaps this is the vehicle for it.' Then it started to come up on my Instagram feed, I would notice things about booking writing workshops coming up and then before you know it, wham, there it was! I was in Glastonbury at the time, peeling away another layer and after a big light bulb moment post-sound healing session in the Goddess temple, in comes an email about a writer's workshop – my tummy turned and I knew that was my gut saying 'do it'. The following week a post about the workshop came up – I literally couldn't get away from the signs, they were everywhere. So

I did the workshop, wrote a book proposal and got a book contract, all in the space of 6 months – this book birthed 15 months after that. Look at that for manifesting, noticing the signs and taking action!

MOMENTS OF AWE

As you embark on opening up to the Universe and its energy, you will encounter many moments of awe and wonder. This comes in the form of synchronicities and/or intentions manifested – both big and small. Moments of awe are small moments in time where you may utter the words 'WTF' or even 'Wow, that's weird' – even though it's not weird, and it always makes complete sense because it's simply your manifestation arriving on your doorstep or an awe-inspiring moment that your positive energy has drawn in. It's a moment when you are bowled over by the magic, the timing and miraculous delivery of the message. One of the biggest, most mind-boggling mini miracles that I have ever experienced was with Michelle Zelli in Ibiza, where we had travelled to explore some shamanic teachings. We had set our intention before we went to Ibiza to go with whatever the Universe delivered. We stayed in our hearts, followed our gut and held on to our pants. We were due to meet an amazing ancient shamanic tribe from the heart of the Amazon that night, and before we did we went to a gorgeous vegan restaurant, set in the Ibizan countryside. As I sat there in awe of the décor, menu and company, I turned to my left and right there on the next table was my other mentor,

Marisa Peer. WTF!? What are the chances of being in another country, sitting at the table next to Marisa, while I'm next to my other mega influence Michelle? It was pure alchemy; being shown my two mentors alongside each other was just magic. And here I am writing a book about both of their processes combined, which have formed my process and journey. Now if that isn't a miracle, coincidence or synchronicity, I don't know what is. That weekend continued to be filled with a whole host of mini miracles, magic events and more, to the point that as I departed the White Island, I knew there was something so much greater at play and they were my rewards for letting go of the old and welcoming the new. Magic awaits you too; look and you will find. Let go of what no longer serves you and make way for the new. You deserve it, you matter. As I say, or even sing, to my Feminine Superpower ladies, 'Get out of your own way.' Start to notice the amazing coincidences and signs – the more you look, the more you will find.

SIGNS

LOOK AND YE SHALL FIND

You rush through life at such a rate you barely have time to stop and take in the world around us. I'm asking you, as of today, to reduce the speed on the speedometer. When you do, you will begin to notice the signs that the Universe is sending you, either in the form of synchronicities or moments of awe but also in the form of animals, signs, symbols and numbers.

Do you ever have those moments when you are sitting peacefully and a little bird comes and sits by you, looks you in the eye and flies off? That's a sign in the form of a Universal messenger. Sounds completely bizarre, I know, but it's true! When I have a visitor, I look up the spiritual symbol of the visitor in one of my books (or on the internet) and, lo and behold, either they symbolise something I am feeling at the time or are showing me what I need to do.

Numbers and numerology are a popular way of noticing what vibration you are vibrating at. It is thought that each number has a cosmic frequency and vibration. When you start to notice master numbers such as 11, 111, 22, 222, 33, 333, 44, 444, 555, 666 (the devil!), 777, 888, 999 (not just the police!), you are being sent a message and something magical is occurring. Start to notice when such numbers appear and look up the meaning in a numerology book; you'll be surprised at what you find out.

DREAMS

Dreams are another great way of receiving messages and letting go of old emotions. They are the gateway to your soul and a place that your soul talks to you. When I remember a dream, I always explore what I felt in that dream and how that relates to what is going on in my awake life. For example, if I had a fearful dream I would explore where I am feeling fear in my life and what it is I am in fear of. Dreams create a place where we can offload and process unresolved and unprocessed emotions from our day-to-day life. I found the more I opened my mind, the more vivid my dreams became and they are now a valuable tool to getting a deeper understanding of what and how I feel in my awake life. But what if you don't dream? Don't worry, but that can be a sign you're shutting down your emotions because when we dream we feel and embody emotions. Explore what emotions you don't want to acknowledge and work on feeling these emotions and acknowledging they exist in you and need space to be felt. Remember when we shut down a negative emotion such as anger, we shut down positive emotions too, like love and joy. What are your dreams telling you?

Start to notice the magic that awaits you. As Roald Dahl said, 'Only people that believe in miracles, see miracles'. Well, I now believe in miracles, I have irrefutable evidence that when I align my thoughts and intentions, magic appears. It's over to you now, go and find some miracles, they are everywhere; just set your intention and miracles will appear. Happy exploring, I told you this was fun!

There really is so much magic out there in the world and inside of you that you have yet to experience and tap in to. You will have uncovered and realised just how magical you are from me telling you so and after your mind detox, I'm sure you're really beginning to feel it too. What you have experienced on your journey with me is just a drop in the ocean of what you are capable of and how much you can change your life. Continue to work on the areas we have discussed, letting go of old memories and limiting beliefs (they are there to be upgraded), changing the world inside you and around you and taking daily actions to fulfil your life's purpose. Your sparkle has returned, you have a spring in your step and you can now see a big light at the end of the tunnel – that light is you, your future you.

What have I discovered?

What do I want to change?

What do I want to create?

☆

'Lay bare your *magnificence* for
the world to see.'

Creating Your Future

chapter nine

Darling,

It's time to dust off your glad rags, spruce up your hair and shine like you have never shone before!

I'll support you every step of the way and together we will fulfil your dreams.

Deal?

Shine on, Sister!

Love

Your Self-Esteem

'There is no greater power than a woman determined to rise, shine her light, use her voice and take over the world!'

An anonymous quote reinterpreted by Me.

Well, well, well … here we are … you, me and the Universe, all together, completely aligned and ready for the big unveil. You have set out what you want, you feel it, you believe it, now it's time to sit back, put your feet up and have a cup of tea. Your work is essentially done.

As you grow and set your sights on bigger goals, triggers may come but you now have the toolbox to navigate and sail through life's ups and downs. You can choose how you handle a situation, you are powerful – no longer powerless. Remember, if a trigger comes up, go to the feeling, ask yourself *how old* you feel and *when* you felt this feeling as a child. Go back to the instance and rewrite the scene, rescue or reassure the little one inside that she is loved and safe, hear what she has to say and respond with compassion and unconditional love. Work with your inner child every day – this is a life-long partnership between the two of you and like all relationships, they take work. Keep your eye on the prize and take daily steps towards what it is you want.

Remember, the Universe NEVER makes mistakes and as a trigger comes, it is perfectly placed and has a lesson and gift in it. Look on with curiosity and learn from the situation, however the situation might feel at the time. There is always a gift, look for it and apply this mindset to life, it will change the way you see a situation.

As you break out of your shell, you'll find that you randomly start throwing out clothes, cleaning and rearranging your home. This is completely normal. As you reorganise your internal layout, so do you your external – it's that mirror again. As I healed and let go, I found the way I ate, dressed and shopped all changed. I now always buy consciously and ethically. The same applies to my make-up and cosmetics, they all got an upgrade to vegan, natural, organic products much like my food (although I'm not 100% vegan, I eat mostly a plant-based diet). As you take care of you, your mind and your body, you take care of the planet. With every vibration you raise, the vibration around you rises – it's a ripple effect, just like kindness and love. Love breeds love. Birth it like you have never before, make love and birth it here and now.

Here's the *Born to Shine* guide to life:

☆ *HONOUR YOUR EMOTIONS – Let your feeling flow so that you can grow. A good cry waters your soul. Let it flow and let it go! When we don't let it go, it leads to dis-ease in your body. No time for that when you are living a high vibe life! Don't push down the feelings or numb them out, honour them, allow the tears to flow and the anger to surface in a healthy and safe way. If you need a duvet day and Netflix following a long meditation, then I prescribe that to you!*

☆ *LIVE CLEAN – Chuck it out – you know the power of a good detox – this includes your emotions, what you put in your body, on your body, your environment and what you consume in terms of media, food and literature (this includes social media!). Match your high vibe life with high vibe choices on every level!*

☆ *PRACTISE GRATITUDE – Aside from being thankful for your new dream-filled life, think of three things you are thankful for each morning or evening. Gratitude is the antidote to fear and anger. Thank you, thank you, thank you!*

☆ *SELF-LOVE – You are love, a walking talking symbol of love – always use kindness and compassion towards yourself. Love is the answer to everything and it starts with yourself and spreads out beyond. This is about using kindness and compassion towards yourself, while taking time to self-care.*

☆ *MEDITATE – Find your groove, pick a way that works for you. Just 5 minutes in the morning every day, will change the way you tackle your day. Ohmmm…kapowww! The benefits are profound. It's a game changer and will allow you the time to tune in to what you're 'feeling' instead of filling your time with an activity that numbs it out.*

☆ YOGA – *Stretch, move and calm your body. It is the greatest complement to your busy life. When you slow the body down, you accelerate your superpower abilities! Move it, stretch it, work it! You store emotions in your bodies so when you stretch you allow breath into the areas that need it and let go of what no longer serves you.*

☆ ROLL WITH YOUR CYCLE – *Moon cycles, planetary shifts and your own menstrual cycle. When you are in tune with these, like the seasons, you will honour your mind and body at an even greater level. This is a serious tool to add to your arsenal, your own built-in, unique superpower. Blow me down with a feather!*

☆ EAT TO NOURISH – *Food is the fuel for your mind, body and spirit. The food you eat matches the way you feel about yourself. High vibe food = high vibe living. Plant-based food is a great place to start – fill your plate up with the Sun's energy. That's not to say no meat but limit meat intake and only buy from organic, well-sourced farms. Too many people use food as a way of self-harming so ask yourself, is what I'm eating healing or hurting my body? Am I hungry or am I using this to numb out a feeling? When we bring conscious awareness to our eating patterns, you can see how to, and how not to, fuel your body based on what it needs and wants.*

☆ LOVE YOUR EXERCISE – *It's time to move it and groove it like you did as a kid. Whatever gets your body active is great! Every woman knows how good she feels when she gets her body moving! Stop punishing your body and doing exercise you hate, start loving you and your body and treating it like you do.*

☆ *GET SOME SLEEP – As you live your high vibe life it's even more important to catch some 'A' grade Zzzz each night! Your body heals when you sleep – fact. Not just that but it's when you sleep your mind travels and you get clear connection to your superpowers direct from your soul! Our minds let go of emotions and process information while we sleep. It is key to living a long and healthy life. It's important to go to bed at a reasonable hour and sleep no less or more than 7-8 hours. Annnd Shleeep!*

Take your time, baby steps to integrate these practices into your life. This is about creating a new way of living – high vibe life for a high vibe being! Here's to you and your future, your new life, your journey, I'm right by your side as your number one cheerleader. Go girl!!!

Some more tips and tricks to add to your bag of magic:

☆ *ESSENTIAL OILS – They work like a beaut. Why? When you smell an essential oil, the particles immediately activate your neural sensors creating a reaction. Much like our thoughts vibrate at a certain frequency, so does a smell; Damask Rose Oil has the highest measured frequency of any essential oil at 320Hz. Sniff it up and raise your vibe immediately.*

☆ *WATER – Drink plenty of water and ideally pick a source that is clean and unpolluted with toxins such as fluoride; they clog up your third eye and we wouldn't want that now, would we. Why drink water? Well, as you know your body is over 60% water, so there's the obvious reason other than keeping you alive! Another reason is because this is how one moves energy around the body, keeping the flow, the chi, going so energy doesn't get lodged or stuck behind any nooks and crannies.*

☆ *TAROT CARDS – Now that you know there is life out there, you can tune in to the powers that be. The angels, spirit guides and our ancestors are there waiting to give you guidance and even more wisdom than you already possess. I use them when I have a question to ask and need an answer to something. Occasionally I get a message I don't want, like WAIT... which frustrates me but it's always right – I just don't like to hear it. I also use them before a client session to give me some information about them ahead of working with them. Find a way that works for you, it's like your ethereal encyclopaedia.*

☆ *CANDLES – I love to light a candle, not just because they smell nice and look pretty. They are grounding, reminding us that we have a fire that burns within us when we ignite it. I always light one before I sit down to be creative, it's like a reminder that I'm calling in protection and inspiration from above. It reminds my subconscious mind that I'm held. Create a ritual for yourself that evokes the same feeling, maybe add some incense. I also set this up before I meditate or do yoga. It readjusts my focus to inside of me, rather than externally.*

☆ *ALTARS – I didn't know what these were until I started to follow other spiritual teachers and realised how valuable an altar is. Much like a candle, it reminds you of your intention, it's a sacred and held space where you call in the magic of the Universe. Mine has all the elements in it, I have stones and seashells from the beach, feathers from the park, water from the White Spring in Glastonbury, candles, a place to light incense, my tarot and angel cards. I always travel with a mini altar so I can retreat to this space wherever I am in the world. Virtual altars are great too, a place in your mind that you go to ask questions, speak to your inner child. Find that space to heal and use it, wherever that might be.*

☆ *YOUR ETHERIC TRIBE – This comes in the form of angels, archangels, Black Madonna, Mother Mary, Jesus Christ, Goddess Kali, Durga and many more. Call the tribe in, invite them around that place in your mind. Depending on what you need at the time they all have different characteristics and strengths to offer. This is real, you can't see them but they can see you and when they are called, they want to help. Trust me. You're not alone, we are held by the most wonderful energies, you've just got to believe it and use it.*

You now have a host of tools and you understand why they will work for you. Always walk with the knowledge that you are limitless and boundless, and that everything and anything is possible. Tap into your potential because you are infinitely powerful. Never ever be limited by another's limiting beliefs or limitations. I was a victim of my ignorance about the

Universe and its magic. You aren't, there is no hiding now. I am a manifestation of my dreams; once I let go of the old, I created a new life. This book is the symbol of that growth and belief in myself, something that five years ago I didn't have. It took 35 years to learn it and now I live it.

Your mission, now that you have subscribed to your limitless lifestyle, is to be creative every single day. When you are creative, your soul is singing, your heart is open and you lay bare your magnificence for the world to see and feel. You were born to share a creative gift, go forth and share, practise and work at it and find that thing, that hobby, that act that shines your light, makes you feel whole inside, and do it every god-damn day, without fail. You owe it to yourself. Let your heart sing and your soul dance to the tune of your creativity and the music that is life.

Continue to grow, darling, don't stop now. You're doing so well. Life is yours for the taking. Travel, grow, glow. Seek inspiration, however that comes – through high vibe music, concerts, films, books, adventure, or travelling the world on a shoe-string. Do it. Do it now. Today. Every day. When we are inspired we are in-spirit.

And finally, always believe, believe in yourself, believe in the process. Believe there is something out there bigger than you, and that is the Universe. Believe that you can do it, believe you always could, you just momentarily forgot how. Believe because what else are you going to do? Believe, be-live. Live. Love. Life. You've got this. I believe in you.

What more have I discovered?

What else do I want to change?

What else do I want to create?

☆

'Go forth.

Shine on.

Be you.'

And

Finally...

Darling,

No more playing small. No more keeping quiet. Open up your throat, shout from the rooftops. The planet wants to hear and see you, your message and your gift, and so do I!

Shine on, Sister!

Love

Your Self-Esteem

'She fell. She crashed. She broke.
She cried. She crawled. She hurt.
She surrendered and then...
She rose again.
In all her glory she rose up
like a phoenix from the flames
and showed the world her light'

Nausicaa Twila quote reinterpreted by Me.

There we are, our journey together comes to a close (for now). Let's toast your magnificence as it radiates out, blinding those who choose not to look towards the light. You are beaming, you are shining like the brightest star in the night sky, and my goodness you deserve it. Just like you were the apple of your parents' eye (even if you didn't feel it) you are that sparkling star in the Universe's third eye. Hold that space, you are part of this thing called life, a unique and exquisitely formed human being who is playing a part of this infinitely powerful and limitless Universe. Don't ever let anyone tell you that you aren't magic because you now know just how magical you are.

What now? The world awaits. But in terms of us, don't forget you have access to the free resources in the back of this book and on my website. You'll have guided meditations, hypnoses and more to continue your growth and use as go-to tools if and when you need them. This is only the beginning of your magnificence. You've only just started and just look at you already.

You can reach out to me on Facebook and become part of the sisterhood where you can connect with like-minded women on a mission to take over the world. Plus, there is my online course if you want more from me – live hypnoses, untapped access to me so that I can cheerlead you all the way to greatness – then, of course, we can work 1 to 1, just me, you and the Universe together again, growing, building and manifesting an empire where you are Queen of your life.

Don't forget about the *Born to Shine* guide to life. Print it out from the resources and live by that. You have this book to refer to; always go back to it and remind yourself why you are doing what you do, why such things work and what you're going to get by doing the work.

For now, though, it's been a beautiful journey. I have loved every minute of our time together, may we meet again on planet Earth or up there amongst the moon and stars. Now off you go, you've got work to do. You were born to shine and now you know it. Shine on, Sister.

love Cat

x

I discovered.

I changed.

I created.

BOOK RESOURCES

Thank you for allowing me to guide you through your journey. I would be honoured to continue working with you. Are you ready for more?

Please head to my website for the *Born to Shine* complimentary book resources, including your accompanying guided meditations for each chapter:

www.catraincock.com/book-resources

☆ 1 to 1 Coaching with Cat

You can work with me 1:1 – to set up a complimentary telephone consultation please head to the following and contact me:

www.catraincock.com/work

☆ Born to Shine Sisterhood Group

Check out my Facebook group and join me and other like-minded women for live hypnoses, exclusive videos, guided meditations and much more. Head to Facebook and look up the 'Born to Shine Sisterhood' group.

☆ Podcast – Honestly Cat

Plug in to my bi-weekly podcast, available on iTunes. The place to hear from authentic, real women who are shining their light. This is your space to be inspired.

www.catraincock.com/podcast

☆ Get on my list

Receive complimentary teachings, hypnoses and gifts by signing up to my newsletter at:

www.catraincock.com/book-resources

☆ Stay in touch

Website: www.catraincock.com
Email: hello@catraincock.com
Facebook: @iamcatraincock
Instagram: @catraincock

#borntoshinebook

Shine on, Sister

OTHER WAYS TO SHINE

☆ Michelle Zelli

Michelle Zelli, Human Potentialist & Coach. Blending a Blue Chip / MD background with spiritual wisdom and cutting edge science, Michelle is relentless in her mission for self-mastery and teaching others to find their own powerful path. She has become a secret weapon for celebrities and CEOs worldwide.

www.michellezelli.com

☆ Rapid Transformational Therapy (RTT)

If you are interested in training in the Marisa Peer process, Rapid Transformational Therapy (RTT) or want to find a therapist near you, please head to the following websites:

www.rapidtransformationaltherapy.com

www.findatherapist.marisapeer.com/FAT

HELPING OTHERS TO SHINE

Just like I help other women to shine, you can too. When I embarked on my journey of self-discovery, I had a deep calling to share my journey with others so that they could change their life and experience the same level of happiness I do. You too can inspire other women, not just by leading by example but by sharing the work that you have done on yourself and gifting this book so that they can learn how to shine.

For every woman who does the work on herself, we raise the vibration of the planet and show the younger generation how it is done. Whether it is a friend, mother, auntie or soul sister, you can help them to change their life so that our daughters, god-daughters, nieces, aspiring mermaids and mini goddesses can rise up and shine their light for the world to see.

Here we glow

RECOMMENDED READING LIST

Here is a list of books that were influential in my growth:

- ☆ *Light is The New Black* By Rebecca Campbell
- ☆ *The Power of Intention* By Dr Wayne W. Dyer
- ☆ *Rise Sister Rise* By Rebecca Campbell
- ☆ *Love Your Lady Landscape* By Lisa Lister
- ☆ *Mastering Your Mean Girl* By Melissa Ambrosini
- ☆ *The Universe Has Your Back* By Gabby Bernstein
- ☆ *The Goddess Revolution* By Mel Wells
- ☆ *The Power of Now* By Eckhart Tolle
- ☆ *The Untethered Soul* By Michael A. Singer
- ☆ *The Biology of Belief* By Bruce H. Lipton
- ☆ *You Are The Placebo* By Dr Joe Dispenza

Look up these books and see which ones resonate with you and draws you in - that will be the right book at the right time.

ABOUT CAT

Cat Raincock is your typical girl-next-door Londoner, women's mentor, podcaster, and author.

She didn't always have this life: the amazing family, beautiful home, fulfilling career... in fact, just five years ago her life looked and felt very different. She was newly married and had two children but felt empty. Despite ticking the boxes that society told her would equal happiness, she felt lost, stuck, overwhelmed, underwhelmed and desperately wanted more from life. Was this it?! She made a commitment to herself to change her life and has dedicated the last few years to her. She faced her shadows, looked back over her childhood and learnt why she was feeling like she did. Lightbulb moment! She has never looked back.

It's her mission to empower women and she is starting with you. Everyone is entitled to a big life upgrade. Her story is here to show women that there is hope, you do matter and there is more to life than what you are experiencing. It's time to align your life so that you can become the woman you were meant to be before the world told who you should be.

#borntoshinebook